COLLINS GEM
ANTIQUE
MARKS

a mine of information

COLLINS GEM
BIBLE
GUIDE

a mine of information

COLLINS GEM
Body
LANGUAGE

a mine of information

COLLINS GEM
CARD
Games

a mine of information

COLLINS GEM
CRICKET

a mine of information

COLLINS GEM
DIETING
FAT

a mine of information

COLLINS GEM
DOGS

a mine of information

COLLINS GEM
FIRST AID

a mine of information

COLLINS GEM
INTERNET

a mine of information

COLLINS GEM
PREDICTING

a mine of information

COLLINS GEM
Ready
REFERENCE

a mine of information

COLLINS GEM
SHARKS

a mine of information

COLLINS GEM
WHALES
& DOLPHINS

a mine of information

COLLINS GEM
WHISKY

a mine of information

COLLINS GEM
WORD

COLLINS GEM

D1570748

MUSICAL INSTRUMENTS

Philip Dodd and Ian Powling

**Consultant:
Dr Lucien Jenkins**

HarperCollins*Publishers*

Consultant **Lucien Jenkins** founded *Early Music Today* magazine in 1993 and was appointed editor of *Music Teacher* magazine in 1996. He was a consultant with the Qualifications and Curriculum Authority, preparing the ground for revising music content of the National Curriculum.

Philip Dodd is a jazz pianist and the author of the *Encyclopedia of Singles* and *The Rock Book*, and compiler with Dora Lowenstein, of *The Rolling Stones: A life On The Road*.

Ian Powling is a former songwriter and drummer who now enjoys exploring the Brazilian and jazz repertory for guitar.

HarperCollins*Publishers*
Westerhill Road, Bishopbriggs,
Glasgow, G64 2QT
www.collins-gem.com

First published 2000

Reprint 10 9 8 7 6 5 4 3 2 1 0

© The Foundry Creative Media Co. Ltd 2000

ISBN 0 00 472498-4

Created and produced by Flame Tree Publishing, part of
The Foundry Creative Media Co. Ltd
Crabtree Hall, Crabtree Lane, London, SW6 6TY

Printed in Italy by Amadeus S.p.A.

 # Contents

Introduction

MUSIC HAS been a part of every culture for many thousands of years and making music has long been considered an art form. Through the centuries, music has served many purposes, from primitive rituals to lavish court entertainment, ancient religious services to modern secular music. The development of musical instruments is a fascinating story: from the earliest music-making devices right through to the varied and sophisticated instruments being made and played today. Instrument-making is a highly skilled craft and pieces are often beautiful creations, works of art in themselves. Today, many early instruments are valued collectors' items.

Whether you are a fan of jazz and blues, classical or pop music, an active musician or a passive listener, *Collins Gem Musical Instruments* will take you on a journey of discovery through the development and playing techniques of more than 100 instruments. For some, many of the instruments in this book will be new or unusual, so an example of the instrument in performance in a range of genres is given, as well as variations on the instrument from around the globe.

The Elements of Music

IN THIS BOOK key musical terms are defined in the glossary on page 182. To give a basic background to these terms, the following is a brief description of the basic elements of Western music. Traditionally they fall into three areas: rhythm, melody and harmony.

• **Rhythm** is the grouping of sounds in a regular pulse. The basic unit of rhythm is the beat, which occurs at regular intervals. For a piece of music, the duration of a beat is given a name e.g. minim, crotchet or quaver. The time signature tells you how many beats to the bar and the duration of the beat, e.g. 4/4 (four crotchets to the bar) for most popular music and 3/4 for waltzes.

• Commonly called a tune, a **melody** is a succession of notes in a particular rhythm that rise and fall in patterns. Written melodies are arranged as notes on five lines call a **staff**; notes with pitches higher or lower than those on a staff are marked on leger lines – short horizontal lines above or below the staff. The pitch of a note says how high or low it is, named by letters – A, B, C, D, E, F or G – which correspond to the white notes on a piano. The extra notes of the **octave**, the black notes on a piano, are called **sharp** or **flat**, e.g. B♭ (B flat).

• A **harmony** is the combination of notes to make a **chord**. Harmony also tells us about the mood and where we are in the music. The **intervals**, or distances, between notes that comprise a chord give the chord its own character such as 'major' or 'minor'. The **key** of a piece of music determines which chords are used. When written, the key signature uses symbols for sharp (#) and flat (♭) to show the precise pitches of notes for the key.

PERCUSSION INSTRUMENTS
Introduction

THERE IS something elemental and powerful about percussion. Since time immemorial people believed that the sound of a gong, a drum or a rattle could scare away evil spirits and attract good fortune. Along with the voice, it is one of the earliest – and, at one level, one of the simplest – ways of music making: beating a stick against a drum, tapping a foot, or clapping hands. There is rhythm, to varying degrees, within all of us.

Playing percussion can be intensely physical, with the hands acting directly on to the instrument (on the congas, say), or with the sticks or beaters becoming extensions of the body. But percussion is not just about making a noise and hitting things.

At its finest there is a beauty of precision and a visual excitement that can take your breath away: the castanet work of a flamenco dancer, a vibes player skipping over the metal bars, a rock drummer thundering round his battery of tom-toms and cymbals, an orchestral percussionist 'pealing' the tubular bells.

There are two main types of percussion instrument:
- Indefinite pitch: where no specific note is produced, e.g. tambourine, maracas, triangle.
- Definite pitch: where the instrument is tuned to specific notes, e.g. xylophone, timpani, steel drums.

Sometimes a basic groove can come from a percussion instrument as ordinary as a milk bottle hit with a screwdriver (on Bob Marley's 'Jamming'); at the other end of the scale the composer Edgard Varèse created a work called *Ionisation* in 1931 that calls for no fewer than 13 performers, each playing an array of multiple percussion.

Bass Drum

THE DOMINANT FEATURE of every military band is its big bass drum. Throughout the history of percussion instruments, this drum has been the mainstay of time-keeping, whether it is used for a marching army or in a late-twentieth century heavy metal band.

Early versions of the bass drum (it was certainly known in Asia around 3500 BC) were often gigantic constructions, although the world's largest bass drum record is claimed by one with a diameter of over 3 metres: built for Disneyland by Remo of Hollywood. Both sides of the drum have heads, so the marching player can strike the heads with felt-covered drumsticks with alternate hands. The resulting boom has great power, but the drum is not really suited to rapid notes or drumrolls.

In an orchestra, the bass drum is usually held in a tilting position on a stand that can be adjusted for a better angle of attack. A smaller bass drum – struck by a foot pedal – is a staple of the drum kit (ideal as an advertisement hoarding, like Ringo Starr's Ludwig bass drum for The Beatles). In the late 1960s and early 1970s there was a vogue for using a double bass drum kit inspired by Cream's Ginger Baker.

PERFORMANCE

OUTSIDE MILITARY BANDS, Berlioz notably used the bass drum in his 1827 overture *Les Francs Juges*. A century and a half later the bass drum was providing a heartstopping, chest-heaving beat on dance tracks like New Order's 'Blue Monday' and Roxy Music's 'Dance Away'.

CONNECTIONS

The **kendang**, central to Indonesian gamelan music, is also a double-headed drum but with a much wider barrel-shaped body. The **odaiko**, also double-headed, is used in Japanese theatrical music.

The percussion section of a modern orchestra.

Castanets

CASTANETS ARE CLOSELY associated with the musical and dance traditions of Spain, but they are by no means unique to the Iberian peninsula. Clappers were played as far back as Sumerian times, and the Egyptians fashioned wood, bone and ivory into forearms and hands that worked like castanets.

Castanets are disc-shaped pieces of wood hollowed out on one side with a loop of cord holding each pair together. Although the word castanet derives from *castaña*, the Spanish for 'chestnut', they are most frequently made from other woods, including walnut and ebony.

In performance, the loop is placed round the thumb or middle finger, so the two halves can be snapped together by the palm and fingers.

Flamenco dance virtuosos like Antonio Gades and Cristina Hoyos have the ability to manipulate the castanets with spellbinding speed and breathtaking dexterity to complement the rhythm of their footwork. In the orchestra, for ease of use, the castanets are mounted on the end of a stick and held apart by elastic.

Decorated claves.

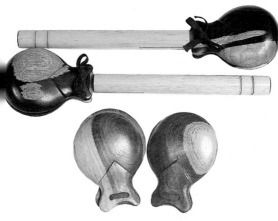

PERFORMANCE

CASTANETS CAN be heard to good effect in Maurice Ravel's *Alborada del Gracioso* and Manuel de Falla's *The Three-Cornered Hat*, as well as William Walton's gentle pastiches 'Tango-Pasodoblé' and 'Noche Espagnole' from *Façade*.

CONNECTIONS

Other wood-on-wood instruments include the **claves**, two wooden sticks some 20 cm long, much used in Cuban music (especially the rumba) and the **wood block**, an oblong rectangle with a resonating slit hit by a drumstick to produce a penetrating click, favoured by Dixieland and ragtime bands.

Congas

T HE RHYTHM SECTIONS of Latin American bands are enhanced by a range of propulsive percussion instruments, of which the largest are the congas, the single-headed drums that found their way from Africa to Cuba and beyond.

The congas – also known as tumba drums – have an upright barrel shape: the body of the drum is made of hard wood or fibreglass, open at the bottom and supported by four legs. A vellum or calfskin head is held tight on to the body below the actual level of the drumhead, giving the player unencumbered access to all parts of the head. As with the tabla, the skill lies in using all parts of the hand, including the flat palm and the fingertips.

Generally used in pairs with different pitches, the congas are frequently complemented in Latin American line-ups by:

Cuban drummers with their congas.

- Timbales: a pair of high-pitched metal-shelled drums, played with sticks and mounted on a stand with a cowbell.
- Bongos: two small bucket-shaped wooden drums, joined by a metal bar and played with the thumb and fingers.

PERFORMANCE

THE CONTRAST and interplay between the congas and the timbales is evident on Santana's 'Se A Cabo', and 'Oye Como Va' (a number by timbale virtuoso Tito Puente). Little Feat's conga player Sam Clayton appeared on 'Spanish Moon', while Haircut 100 featured the congas on 'Favourite Shirts'.

CONNECTIONS

Other single-headed drums include the **tom-tom**, a native American Indian drum, and the **atumpan**, a traditional Ghanaian drum, which is a kind of hybrid between the bongos and the congas.

Cymbals

WE KNOW THAT the clashing of 'loud' and 'well-tuned' cymbals were familiar to the writers of the Psalms, but their origins are unclear: certainly they were first used in the East, possibly in Assyria or Turkey, from where they reached the orchestras of Western Europe during the eighteenth century.

Cymbals are concave plates of brass or bronze, held at the centre – either by leather handles or a pole – so that the edges of the metal can vibrate. Their manufacture remains a craft full of closely guarded secrets and tradition: the present-day Zildjian cymbal company is descended from a long line of Turkish cymbal-makers.

There are now hundreds of varieties to select from, particularly for use on a drum kit, including:

- The crash: a bright cymbal with a fast crescendo.
- The sizzle: with half a dozen rivets set loosely in the cymbal.

- The ride: a ringing cymbal for driving the rhythm along.
- The hi-hat: two smaller cymbals clashed together by pedal action.

For alternative effects the cymbals can be played with drum sticks, timpani sticks or wire brushes – or even recorded backwards, as The Beatles did on 'Strawberry Fields Forever'.

PERFORMANCE

THE CLIMAXES of many of Gustav Mahler's symphonies use to splendid effect the power of the clashing cymbal, especially his Fifth. Led Zeppelin drummer John Bonham laid down a sheet of sound on tracks like 'Rock and Roll'; compare the skittering cymbal play of jazz drummer Jon Christensen on Keith Jarrett's 'Questar' or the funky hi-hat technique of Isaac Hayes' 'The Theme from *Shaft*'.

CONNECTIONS

Antique cymbals – also known as finger cymbals or crotales – are only a few centimetres in diameter: they provide the only percussion in Claude Debussy's *Prélude à l'après-midi d'un faune*.

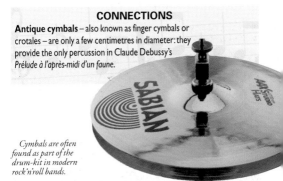

Cymbals are often found as part of the drum-kit in modern rock'n'roll bands.

Drum Kit

T HE DRUM KIT is so much a part of contemporary music that it's easy to forget it's a relatively recent invention, even though the separate elements that make it up often date to antiquity. In the 1900s, a need emerged for a way of playing various percussion instruments, ideally while sitting down; this need was driven in the main, though not exclusively, by jazz drummers.

The resulting set-up was originally known as 'traps' (short for contraption – a term still used by some players) and was common by the 1920s in Dixieland and dance bands. By the 1950s the basic combination of instruments and implements had stabilised:

- Bass drum (smaller than in military bands), struck by a floor-pedal beater.
- Snare drum.
- Different sized tom-toms and cymbals mounted either on the drum or a floor stand.
- Hi-hat cymbal (two cymbals clashed together by a foot pedal).

Drummers can explore endless variations: double bass drums (Billy Cobham once used three!), additional instruments like wood blocks, as well as a customised mix of drum heads, cymbal shapes or stick weights, so each drummer creates a blend of sounds that becomes his or her personal signature.

Drummers can make up their own kit to produce a variety of sounds.

PERFORMANCE

BILLY COBHAM'S dynamic style can be heard on Miles Davis's *Live-Evil*; compare this with the laid-back reggae groove of Carlton Barrett on Bob Marley's 'No Woman, No Cry' or Buddy Rich's swing on 'Jumpin' at the Woodside'. A classic rock solo by John Bonham is captured on the Led Zeppelin live movie *The Song Remains the Same*.

CONNECTIONS

The street busker's **one-man band** is a wearable drum kit, with foot- or arm-operated bass drum and cymbals, though usually in combination with other instruments such as a trombone.

Gong

THE GONG has played an important role in the theatre and in religious ceremonies – particularly in the Far East and Central Asia, where it is believed to have originated; in Malaysia gongs were long considered a valuable part of any dowry.

Essentially a large round dish of metal with an upturned edge, often with a raised boss at its centre, the gong is hit with a padded drumstick or beater, the heavier the better to build its crescendo of sound. In the classical orchestra, the instrument – about 100 cm in diameter, with a hammered surface and suspended from a frame – is technically called the 'tam-tam' (not to be confused with the tom-tom, see p. 17).

Gongs feature large in the gamelan music of Indonesia; more recently new-age practitioners of 'gong therapy' have used them. Twentieth-century composers also sought to expand its sound range by instructing the percussionist to play the gong with a violin bow (Kryzstof Penderecki) or lower it into water (John Cage).

Gong, or 'tam-tam', from Thailand.

PERFORMANCE

THE ORCHESTRAL GONG can convey a sombre mood, as in François Joseph Gossec's 1791 *Funeral Music for Mirabeau*, or tragic passion, in Giacomo Puccini's *Turandot*. Carl Orff and Olivier Messaien used its power in *Carmina Burana* and *Turangalia-symphonie* respectively. In rock music, Pink Floyd's Roger Waters played a gong during live performances of 'Set the Controls for the Heart of the Sun', while Queen's Roger Taylor rounded off 'Bohemian Rhapsody' with a climactic gong crash.

CONNECTIONS

Gong chimes – the **bonang barung** – form part of the gamelan orchestra, usually lying horizontally in pairs within a wooden frame.

Maracas

THE HUSTLING shaking sound of the maracas is an essential part of Cuban music forms such as the rumba and mambo, although rattles go back to the Egyptians and beyond, in fact predating the drum. Many civilisations have believed that the sound of a rattle can ward off evil spirits or win over benevolent deities.

The sound of the maracas is multi-textured, but the technology is straightforward: a pair of round or egg-shaped containers, made from gourds, wood or plastic, mounted on the end of sticks and filled with anything from beans or pebbles to buttons or lead shot to provide the necessary sizzle. Various techniques are available, including twirling both maracas to create a kind of drumroll, banging one maraca into an open hand, or flicking the shot into the top side of the maracas before letting it fall back to the bottom for a double shuffle.

Bo Diddley's right-hand man, maracas player Jerome Green, was an essential component of the distinctively syncopated sound of Diddley's singles in the 1950s. Mick Jagger was a fan of both men and was rarely without his maracas during early Rolling Stones performances.

PERFORMANCE

CUBAN MARACAS maestro Alberto Valdés stands out on the
Buena Vista Social Club's 'De Camino A La Vereda'; Jerome
Green features on Bo Diddley's 'I'm A Man' and 'Bo Diddley'.
In the *Jeremiah Symphony* Leonard Bernstein has a single
maraca used like a stick to strike a drum.

CONNECTIONS

Other shaken instruments include the **cabaça**, a round gourd with the
beads in a network on the outside, and the **chocallo**, a metal tube filled
with lead shot or peas.

Snare Drum

THE INSISTENT RHYTHM of the snare drum has accompanied war, work and play since antiquity. The Romans marched to its beat, Elizabethan revellers danced to the pipe and tabor and in the days before field telephones, military messages were transmitted via drum calls. In the twentieth century the snare (or side) drum became an essential part of the standard drum kit, and provided the off-beat drive of rock'n'roll.

In its simplest form the snare drum is a small, cylindrical drum covered with parchment. What gives the drum its distinctive sound is the snare: a strip of metal wires, nylon or gut stretched across the bottom of the drum. When the drummer strikes the top skin, the snare vibrates and the high-pitched rattle is able to slice through the loudest of bands and the fiercest of battles.

The military snare drum is hung over the drummer's shoulder, with the drumhead at an angle for ease of access; rolls, flams and paradiddles support the brass or bagpipes. In jazz and rock the rim shot, a smart

Snare, or side, drums.

crack with the stick simultaneously hitting the metal rim and the drumhead, is a frequent device.

PERFORMANCE

A QUINTESSENTIAL drum roll usually starts 'God Save the Queen'; the constant pattern throughout Ravel's *Boléro* is the basis of the music's hypnotic quality. Ace session drummer Steve Gadd studied military drumming: it shows on Paul Simon's 'Fifty Ways to Leave Your Lover'. The Police's Stewart Copeland often used rim shots (with extra echo) on tracks like 'Walking on the Moon'.

CONNECTIONS

The **tenor drum** is a deeper drum with no snares: Hector Berlioz used six in his *Te Deum*. Elizabethan drummers often played the long, narrow **tabor** and a simple pipe at the same time, with the pipe in one hand and the beater in the other.

Steel Drums

THE STEEL DRUM or steelpan is a relatively recent addition to the ranks of percussion instruments. It was first created in Trinidad in the 1930s and 40s, when a plentiful supply of 45-gallon oil drums was available; and it was found that they could be sliced in half, turned upside down and tuned.

Steel band playing in the street.

Creating a finished steel drum involves cutting the pans to size, sinking down the main pan with a sledge-hammer, defining the areas for up to 30 different notes with compass, chalk, hammer and punch, and then hammering each note back up to form a low dome. Each note is carefully tuned – usually by ear. Finally the drum is tempered and painted, or electroplated, ready for players to use sticks with rubber tips.

A complete range of drums form families, either called after choir voices (treble, alto, bass) or traditional instruments (guitar, cello) supported by a rhythm section. The steel orchestra, particularly in the major West Indian carnivals, can require anywhere up to 100 performers, producing a significantly uplifting volume of sound.

PERFORMANCE

AUTHENTIC STEELBAND music from Trinidad and Tobago is provided by 'Calypso Music' by the Samaroo Jets; the rapso style mixing steelband, calypso and social conscience is typified by Brother Resistance's 'Cyar Take Dat'. Crossover appearances include 10cc's cod-Caribbean 'Dreadlock Holiday'.

CONNECTIONS

There are no true relatives of the steel drum, but the performers from the theatre/dance group Stomp have discovered the rhythmic possibilities of **dustbins**, among many other domestic objects.

Tabla

IT IS SAID that the tabla – the double drums that have been a primary instrument in the classical music of northern India, Bangladesh and Pakistan since the end of the eighteenth century – have the power to talk at the hands of a skilled player. Certainly many people consider that the tabla represents the pinnacle of percussive ability.

The tabla consists of two individual drums, each with its own character. The lower is the bayan – or bhaya – usually positioned to the musician's left (the word *bayan* in fact means 'left'), which has a copper shell, somewhat like a kettledrum, and a double-skinned head attached to the drum body by laces. The distinctive off-centre black spot, a patch made from a concoction using flour, iron filings, tamarind juice and other secret ingredients, lies under the fingertips. The smaller drum, the tabla, has a wooden body; its black patch is in the middle of the head.

The two drums lie on cushions, and players, sitting cross-legged, with the drums between their knees, use all parts of the hand

Tabla playing in India.

TABLA 31

– the heel, fingertips, knuckles and nails – to bring out all the expressive quality of the drums.

PERFORMANCE

TABLA MASTER Alla Rakha and his son Zakir Hussain, a founder of Shakti with John McLaughlin, play a rare tabla duet in 'Dhamar'. Talvin Singh merged tabla and drum'n'bass to produce a unique fusion on 'OK'. The Beatles, following their Eastern odysseys, realised the potential of tabla on 'Within You Without You', capturing all its texture and subtlety.

CONNECTIONS

The **kalangu** is a small talking drum that features in the Hausa music of northern Nigeria.

Tambourine

T HE TAMBOURINE is one of the oldest – but one of the most underrated – of all instruments. The version used today has changed little from that used thousands of years ago by the ancient Greeks (which they called the 'timpnon'). Egyptian friezes show tambourines in the hands of women celebrating sacred ceremonies.

Although its construction is simple – a shallow, round wooden frame or hoop, sometimes with a single, taut, parchment head, and circular metal discs set in pairs into the hoop – the tambourine's bright, fluttering jingle can lift a piece of music on its own. The player can shake the tambourine for a constant, rhythmic pulse, use the finger pads to provide a sharp tap, or strike the tambourine on to a knee, leg or open hand; the thumb trill involves moistening the thumb and running it round the edge of the tambourine.

The tambourine has proved particularly versatile throughout its life: as appropriate to the religious rites of

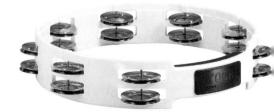

antiquity as it is in folk dancing (particularly in Spain), marching band, who borrowed the instrument from Turkish military music, in rock and pop line-ups, and through generations of Salvation Army bands.

PERFORMANCE

MANOLO BADRENAS'S tambourine provides the essential groove of Weather Report's fusion classic 'Birdland'; Freda Payne's 'Band of Gold' also has a sparkling tambourine track. In Igor Stravinsky's ballet *Petrushka*, the death of the heroine is marked by dropping the tambourine on to the floor, while Debussy's *Ibéria* contains a lengthy, controlled pianissimo trill.

CONNECTIONS

The traditional Irish **bodhrán** is a frame drum, but significantly larger than a tambourine, with no jingles, and played with a wooden beater.

Brazilian percussion maestro Airto Moreira.

Timpani

THE SHAPE of their copper cauldrons suggests the term 'kettledrums'; the Italian name 'timpani', referring to the drumhead, is from the word for a membrane of the ear. Bowl-shaped drums appear in Babylonian drawings, but they first entered Western consciousness when Crusaders brought back examples mounted on horses, camels or carriages.

The essence of the timpani is the fact they can be tuned. Originally this was achieved – with difficulty – by a network of laces, before the introduction of tension screws set round the collar. The problem was that each drum could only play one note at one time, limiting the range or demanding serried ranks of drums. Various people (including Leonardo da Vinci and

Adolphe Sax) tried inventing systems, but only the arrival of pedal tuning in the 1880s finally solved the problem. Now pedals change tunings in a second or two and allow a glissando effect where the note is deliberately allowed to slide up or down.

Their great dynamism and colour, and an ability to create special effects – storms, gunfire in Sergey Prokofiev's *Peter and the Wolf*, a beating heart in Piotr Ilyich Tchaikovsky's *Romeo and Juliet* – has made timpani central to the percussion section.

PERFORMANCE

THE POUNDING timpani in Richard Strauss's *Also Sprach Zarathustra* reached a wide audience through the soundtrack of *2001: A Space Odyssey*; they also provide the malignant dramatic bite in the Uranus movement of Gustav Holst's *The Planets*. Fewer are probably aware of their use in Earth, Wind and Fire's 'Boogie Wonderland' or the trembling undercurrent in Debussy's *Nuages*. The ultimate line-up is Berlioz's requirement for 10 timpanists playing 16 drums in his *Requiem*.

CONNECTIONS

Naqqara are small kettle-drums, with wooden, earthen or metal bodies, used throughout the Middle East and Asia.

Illustration showing a seventeenth-century kettledrum.

Tubular Bells

THE SOUND of a bell can carry for miles, celebrating weddings or warning of attack. Since the great foundry cast bells are weighed in tons, they are less than practical for concert use – hence the invention of the tubular bells by John Hampton of Coventry in the 1880s.

The tubular bells (known in the US as 'chimes') are a portable, efficient way of reproducing the bell sound, although they can never reproduce the sheer power of a genuine belfry. The most common version uses 18 narrow tubes, of the same width but different lengths to produce an octave and a half of individual chromatic notes. They are hung on a frame, damped by a foot-operated pedal to stop the sound and struck by a wooden mallet or a drumstick at the top of the tube.

Other instruments that composers and arrangers can turn to for bell sounds include:

- Handbells, played by teams of ringers.
- Traditional sleigh bells.

The triangle, which also offers a bell-like sound.

- The cowbell, often mounted on top of a drum kit.
- The triangle, which although a single steel rod, has a clear ringing tone with the ability to cut through the largest of orchestras or bands.

PERFORMANCE

NOT SURPRISINGLY, this instrument provides the dénouement of Mike Oldfield's *Tubular Bells*. Tchaikovsky used them to recreate the Kremlin bells in his *1812* Overture; a less predictable appearance is in Chic's 1979 disco classic 'I Want Your Love'. A triangle can be heard insistently throughout Ben E. King's 'Stand By Me', while a cowbell provides the clangorous introduction to The Rolling Stones' 'Honky Tonk Women'.

CONNECTIONS

The **bell tree** – also known as the Chinese pavilion or Turkish crescent – was an ornate pole carrying rows of cup-shaped bells once used in marching bands.

Vibraphone

THE VIBRAPHONE, or vibes, took the metal of the glockenspiel – to all intents and purposes a small xylophone with metal bars – and added metal resonators underneath the bars, kept in motion by an electric motor to provide a quivering, breathy edge to the sound. Originally called the vibraharp, it was invented in the early twentieth century; dance and jazz bands were quick to pick up on its potential.

The glockenspiel ('bell-play' in German), struck with metal beaters, was a relatively simple instrument, and could be carried in marching bands mounted on a rod, when it was known as the bell-lyra. The vibraphone added luscious

Tubaphone.

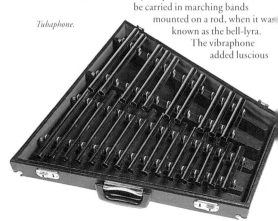

layers of sophistication: the speed of the vibrations could be varied and a sustain pedal controlled the length of the notes. Another incarnation is the tubaphone, which has metal tubes rather than bars, creating a softer sound.

The jazz world has produced the largest crop of virtuoso vibraphone players, most using a pair of mallets in each hand, allowing them to play chords.

Jazz vibraphonist, Lionel Hampton.

PERFORMANCE

THE VIBRANT swing of Lionel Hampton, doyen of jazz vibraphonists, is at its most dazzling on 'Love For Sale', a duet with Oscar Peterson; the elegance of Milt Jackson is on display in the Modern Jazz Quartet's 'Django', while Gary Burton provides lustre for k.d.lang's 'Constant Craving'. A glockenspiel doubles the bass line on Diana Ross's 'Ain't No Mountain High Enough' and adds sparkle to Debussy's *La Mer*.

CONNECTIONS

The **celesta** was a version of the glockenspiel, with wooden resonators and a keyboard, invented in the 1880s – it directly inspired Tchaikovsky to write 'The Dance of the Sugar Plum Fairy' for *The Nutcracker Suite*.

Washboard

A STAPLE INSTRUMENT in zydeco music (black American dance music, also featuring guitar and accordian) and the skiffle bands of the late 1950s, the washboard is one of the most widely used of the instruments that produce their sound by scraping. It is a form of rhythm-making that goes way back. It is also an example of inventive recycling for musical purposes, since the washboard was adapted directly from the domestic corrugated metal board once used in washing clothes.

The washboard as an instrument is based on the same principle as the guiro, a Latin American instrument that uses a stick scraped along the serrated notches carved into a wood block or gourd, except that the washboard creates its sound from the contact between metal and metal – players place thimbles on the ends of their fingers to produce a harder-edged, more rasping sound than the gentler guiro.

Over the years musical washboards have become increasingly elaborate constructions, worn over the shoulder and round the player's neck like an apron and involving Edward Scissorhands-style industrial gloves tipped with metal talons.

PERFORMANCE

WASHBOARD SAM (aka Robert Brown) played with Big Bill Broonzy in the 1940s – 'Play Your Vendor' is a good example of his technique. On the film soundtrack of *The Big Easy*, Terrance Simien & The Mallet Playboys feature some upbeat washboard on 'Oh Yeh Ya!'; the spirit of skiffle is exemplified on Lonnie Donegan's 'My Old Man's a Dustman'. In *The Rite of Spring*, Stravinsky scores a part for the guiro (calling it the 'râpe guero').

CONNECTIONS

The **ratchet** (the football rattle of yesteryear) uses much the same principle as both the washboard and guiro, with its wooden cogs clicking round as the rattle is spun. Richard Strauss calls for one in *Till Eulenspiegel*.

Xylophone

T HE WOOD on wood sound of the xylophone (*xylo* from the Greek for 'wood'), produces a dry, choppy sound that has its roots in much ethnic music: the gamelan orchestras of Indonesia use bamboo, African native instruments used wooden bars set in frames and before that simple logs.

The tuned wooden bars (ideally Honduras rosewood, although some are now synthetic) are the same overall size, but with different-sized recesses underneath to create the pitch of individual notes. Layout of the three to four octaves of notes is as the piano keyboard, with the 'black' notes raised from the 'white' notes. There is no sustain on a xylophone, so players compensate by relying on a tremolando or trill technique; a range of beaters can also brighten or mellow the notes.

The xylophone's role as a concert instrument is primarily due to the Polish player Michael Josef Gusikov, who performed throughout Europe in the 1830s; the instrument enjoyed a vogue for the next 100 years, and was particularly popular during the early days of the gramophone and radio.

PERFORMANCE

CAMILLE SAINT-Saëns used the xylophone to suggest the sounds of skeletons and fossils in *Danse*

The marimba, a relation of the xylophone.

Macabre and *Carnival of the Animals*. Evelyn Glennie pays tribute to the golden age of the instrument in a bravura performance of a 1927 tune, 'Gee Whizz!', with the Black Dyke Mills Band. The xylophone also appears in Tom Jones' version of 'Delilah'.

CONNECTIONS

Originally from Africa, but also adopted by Latin American music, the **marimba** is very similar to the xylophone, but is larger (traditional marimbas are sometimes large enough to have four 'marimberos' playing one instrument at a time) and has resonators beneath the notes to help lengthen the sustain.

BRASS INSTRUMENTS

Introduction

THE VERY NAME 'BRASS' conjures up images of gleaming metal, noble instruments proclaiming fanfares and sending messages through the heat of battle. They are ancient instruments: the trumpet in its purest form – a tube of metal with a mouthpiece but no valves – dates from the second century BC. As well as adding stirring music to the most formal of ceremonies, brass instruments can also be gently comforting, such as the sound of a brass band playing in a park on a summer's afternoon.

What the true brass instruments have in common is the way the sound is produced:

- Air is pushed through the player's lips.
- The lips vibrate inside the cup or funnel-shaped mouthpiece.
- The vibration causes the air in the tube of the instrument to resonate with a distinctive metallic edge.

Vibration of the lips is the key: if you simply blow into a cornet, for example, no musical sound will emerge. The control of the lips – the embouchure – is the fine art of brass playing, and is why it can prove a tiring occupation, not to mention the amount of lungpower involved.

Whether on a bandstand, in the orchestra or in a funk or jazz brass section, the combination of instruments working together is capable of great variety. An orchestra will frequently feature four French horns, a trio each of trumpets and trombones, with a tuba in the bass register. A brass section, like the Muscle Shoals Horns or James Brown's Horny Horns, will mix trumpets and trombones with a range of saxes – which is one of the reasons that the saxophone appears in this section, despite its mongrel mix of brass body and woodwind reed.

Bugle

BEST KNOWN in its military guise, the bugle is one of the simplest of brass instruments in terms of construction, but it is very difficult to play. The single tube of metal has no valves to help create different notes, so players have to do all the work by changing their embouchure – a combination of the tightness of the lips and the amount of air pushed through them.

Although simple tube trumpets date back to the Roman 'tuba', the bugle was a development from circular hunting horns and the usually straight posthorns used by mail-coaches to announce the arrival of the post from the fifteenth century onwards. A coiled horn emerged during the Seven Years' War of the mid-eighteenth century as an army signalling device. By 1800 the English bugle had stabilised as a single loop of copper or brass with a bell at the front, trumpet-style; following the Crimean War the double-loop form became standard.

Because of the restricted range of notes available, bugles were rarely heard outside the context of the army, although orchestral composers did use them to add a whiff of the battlefield. A keyed bugle was patented in 1810, but was shortly replaced by the cornet and the flugelhorn.

Seventeenth-century German musician with a posthorn.

PERFORMANCE

BUGLE CALLS, such as the dignified *Last Post*, have changed
little since the late eighteenth century: Franz von Suppé's *Light
Cavalry Overture* opens with a bugle version of an Austrian
retreat call. Koenig's Posthorn Galop *Post Boy's Return* offers a
rare outing for the posthorn.

CONNECTIONS

Natural trumpets (tubes with no valves) appear in many cultures for
signalling, fanfares and ceremonial purposes, including the Tibetan **dung
chen**, the Chilean **trutruca** and the European **alphorn**.

Cornet

MANY PEOPLE find it difficult to distinguish between the cornet, stalwart of the brass band, and the trumpet, since at first sight the cornet looks like a squat, fat trumpet. Although they share much in common, the essential difference lies in the conical shape of the cornet's body.

Although it works like a trumpet, the conical bore is more like that of a horn, and as a result the cornet possesses a tone which is sweeter, less piercing and more expressive than the trumpet. A deeper mouthpiece also allows players greater versatility: the cornet is a solo instrument of great agility, handling fast, complex runs with nonchalance.

The cornet emerged in the early 1800s as a valved variation on the German posthorn, and even briefly threatened to drive the trumpet out of the symphonic orchestra (an idea strongly supported by playwright George Bernard Shaw). In the nineteenth century, it emerged in the ranks of the brass bands, but it also proved to be a popular solo instrument in early jazz orchestras. The cornet's cousin, the flugelhorn, was a valved bugle that likewise never quite achieved symphonic status (although Ralph Vaughan Williams gave it a prominent role in his Ninth Symphony).

The cornet is one of the key instruments in the traditional brass band.

PERFORMANCE

BRASS-BAND cornet solos are often arrangements of classical pieces – Edward Elgar's *Wand of Youth*, or the plaintive largo from Antonin Dvořák's Symphony No. 9, *From the New World*; there is a rare classical appearance in Gioaccino Rossini's *William Tell*. Early jazz cornet classics include King Oliver's smouldering 'Dippermouth Blues'. The flugelhorn's voice can be heard on Art Farmer's 'Tonk' and Dionne Warwick's 'Walk On By'.

CONNECTIONS

The cornet should not be confused with the **cornett**, a long wooden, often leather-covered tube, played with a brass mouthpiece.

French Horn

THE CIRCULAR shape of the horn is a visual guide to its lineage as a technologically advanced descendant of the traditional hunting horn. The French horn – the name used in English since the 1600s – could more accurately be called the German horn, since that was the true centre of its development.

The distinctive characteristics of the French horn are its constantly growing conical tube ending in a widely flared bell, and a funnel-shaped mouthpiece, both of which contribute to its mellow tone. Much of the history of the horn revolves around players' attempts to control its tuning, using a hand in the bell to change natural notes by a semitone, or relying on sets of cumbersome crooks until the arrival and acceptance of valves during the nineteenth century.

Even with the use of valves, horn players still rely on stopping the bell with a hand to control tuning, helping to create the horn's distant-sounding tone. The sheer playing difficulty has resulted in few concertos for the instrument; orchestral composers rely on at least two pairs working in tandem. Applications in jazz or rock music tend to be found less frequently.

Early example of a French horn.

PERFORMANCE

THE FRENCH HORN'S hunting precedence is referred to in Antonio Vivaldi's 'Winter' movement from *The Four Seasons*; Wolfgang Amadeus Mozart's Horn Concerto No. 4, filled with the scent of the great outdoors, is one of his most bracing works; and sheer power comes from the six horns that play the Jupiter theme in Holst's *The Planets*. George Martin introduced the instrument to The Beatles' 'For No One'; it also features on the Pretenders' 'I Go to Sleep'.

CONNECTIONS

The **shofar** is the traditional Jewish synagogue horn, a ram's horn with a straightened end for the mouthpiece. The **mellophone** was a French horn-like instrument briefly experimented with in jazz.

Sousaphone

A COMMON misconception about the all-American sousaphone is that the instrument was invented from scratch by the March King, John Philip Sousa. In reality Sousa, who was in charge of the US Marine Band in the 1890s, asked Philadelphia instrument makers J. W. Pepper to modify an instrument called the helicon; the company named the final result in his honour.

The helicon was a circular bass tuba created in Vienna in the 1840s; the sousaphone added a detachable bell pointing straight up on early versions, and later in a forward direction. In fact there is no technical need for the bell, now often made of fibreglass: it has a purely decorative role. The player stands inside the circular tubing, which sits coiled like a metal boa constrictor over one shoulder and under the other.

Adjusted and reshaped to improve the ease and convenience of carrying such a heavy bass instrument, the sousaphone is particularly suited for the American marching band. It was also a regular part of Dixieland bands, adding some beef to the bass part in the rhythm section. It is rarely seen in Europe.

PERFORMANCE

THE BEST USE of the sousaphone is of course in Sousa marches – 'The Washington Post' or 'Stars and Stripes' – but it can also be heard in its jazz role, played by Squire Girsback with trumpeter Bunk Johnson on 1940s tracks such as 'Ace in the Hole'. The Temperance Seven's recreation of 1920s jazz also featured the instrument on the 1961 hit 'You're Driving Me Crazy'.

CONNECTIONS

The **serpent**, a similarly curvaceous medieval instrument mixing the wood body of a bassoon with a tuba-style mouthpiece, also featured in marching bands and church choirs in the eighteenth century.

The Saxophone Family

MUSICOLOGISTS SAY, with justification, that the saxophone is a wind instrument because it combines a clarinet mouthpiece and an oboe-like body. But the instrument has always been a slightly uneasy hybrid because of its brass construction – and now sits as comfortably in a brass section as the trumpet or trombone.

In the 1840s Adolphe Sax, the prolific Belgian-born, Paris-based instrument maker, was seeking a way to fill a gap between the clarinet and tenor brass instruments. Using recent improvements in woodwind key construction he developed the instrument, including the upturned bell of the bass clarinet, and began supplying it to military bands. Eventually some classical composers saw its potential (Ravel included sax parts in *Boléro*) but it was the jazz- and dance-band worlds which took it to new heights.

Of the 14 members of the family the most commonly used – apart from the tenor (see p. 56) – are:

- B-flat soprano: usually in its straight version, capable of a strident or other-worldly sound.
- E-flat alto: a creamy tone, often delivered with a soulful feel.
- E-flat baritone: plenty of growling punch in the lower register.

PERFORMANCE

BRANFORD MARSALIS'S soprano sax meanders through Sting's 'Englishman in New York'; John Coltrane is mesmerising on 'My Favorite Things'. Charlie Parker did great things with his alto on be-bop classics like 'Shaw Nuff'; Phil Woods

was pure emotion on Billy Joel's 'Just the Way You Are'. Baritone player Maceo Parker added the oomph to James Brown's 'Papa's Got a Brand New Bag'.

CONNECTIONS

Other saxes include the tiny **sopranino** and the over-sized **bass**. The **stritch** is a straight alto played most notably by Rahsaan Roland Kirk.

British sax star Courtney Pine.

Tenor Saxophone

T HE B-FLAT TENOR saxophone is by far the best known of the saxophone family (see p. 54). After a sluggish start, where its appearance was limited to military bands, a move indoors ensured that its distinctive timbre would create some of the best popular music of the twentieth century – from rock'n'roll to funk, soul to jazz, for which it became a universal icon. When the tenor sax was adopted by the jazz world it was imbued with the dangerous allure the electric guitar held for a different generation.

A tenor sax can deliver both the emotional immediacy and the lack of precision in tuning and note placing which horrified many classical composers and attracted jazz performers. The mouth's direct contact with the instrument allows the saxophonist to communicate as if through speech patterns, bringing his or her personality into direct connection with the audience.

The technique of circular breathing – where the player breathes in through their nose and out through the mouth and instrument simultaneously, using the cheeks like bellows – is challenging but allows long fluid lines of improvisation.

PERFORMANCE

THE FATHER of jazz tenor sax, Coleman Hawkins, is magnificent on his 1939 'Body And Soul', while Lester Young is less florid on 'Shoe Shine Boy'; John Coltrane took up the mantle on 'So What'. Tenor solo highlights in other popular music forms include King Curtis's rock'n'roll honk on the popular Coasters' single 'Yakety Yak'. Raphael Ravenscroft's solo lifted Gerry Rafferty's 'Baker Street'; and Clarence Clemons' driving and emotional sax on Bruce Springsteen's 'Born to Run'.

CONNECTIONS

The **C-melody saxophone** is a smaller version of the B-flat tenor which allows players to play in concert pitch without transposing.

Trombone

THE NOBLE SOUND of the trombone (although Sir Thomas Beecham dubbed it 'a quaint and ancient drainage system') has changed remarkably little since its appearance in the fifteenth century, other than the later addition of a flared bell. It is the only naturally chromatic brass instrument: the slide actually predated the valves trumpeters and horn players use by some four centuries.

Every note on the trombone is played by one of the seven positions of the detachable slide – valve trombones do exist, but purists believe it creates a significant loss of tone. The glissando slide up or down the scale is a unique – and sometimes deliberately comic – effect, but what is perceived of as the trombone's exaggerated expressiveness has limited the classical solo repertory.

The trombone is available in a range of choral voices, including a soprano version, but by far the most common is the tenor, followed by the bass. A late entrant to orchestral music – towards the end of the eighteenth century – it forms the heart of orchestral brass. It was quickly adopted by jazz line-ups (even handling the difficulties of be-bop) and has become an essential ingredient in soul, funk and rock horn sections.

PERFORMANCE

LUDWIG VAN BEETHOVEN'S Fifth Symphony was an early orchestral inclusion; the trombone section also proclaims Richard Wagner's *Ride of the Valkyrie* theme and displays the glissando effect in Stravinsky's ballet music for *Pulcinella*. Jazz trombonist J. J. Johnson is moving on 'Lover Man', while Frank Sinatra's 'I've Got You Under My Skin' features a powerful trombone solo. The instrument has recently had concertos written for it by Iannis Xenakis, Benedict Mason, Toru Takemitsu and Alfred Schnittke. And trombonist Christian Lindbergh includes Sanströt's Motorbike Concerto in his repertory.

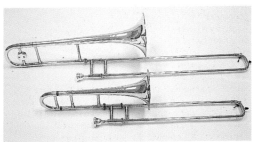

CONNECTIONS

The **sackbut** is a medieval version of the trombone, maybe of Flemish origin, which derives its name from the Old French 'saquier-bouter' (meaning 'draw out-push').

Trumpet

WHEN TUTANKHAMEN'S tomb was re-opened, two metal trumpets were discovered: proof that the trumpet has, for at least 3,000 years, been an instrument of great pomp. Court trumpeters were held in high esteem through to the 1600s. The instrument experienced a decline in popularity during the Classical era but began to rise again in the twentieth century. The instrument really found its *raison d'être*, however, with the arrival of jazz.

Common to all trumpets is a cylindrical metal bore, flared at the end. In the same way as other brass instruments, the trumpet's brilliant flourish is produced through air being

vibrated by the player's embouchure – like blowing a raspberry, except putting the tongue behind the front teeth. Until the fifteenth century different notes could only be produced by tightening the embouchure, but thereafter additional loops, crooks, slides and valves were gradually added to the trumpet.

Left: Dizzy Gillespie;
Right: another of Miles Davis's instruments, the flugelhorn.

Following various tunings, the B-flat trumpet had become the norm by 1900. The three valves are pushed down to divert the air into separate loops; played in combination they can create every regular note, but high ones are still difficult. A plastic or wooden mute, placed in the bell of the trumpet, technically deadens the sound, but produces a haunting, plaintive sound.

PERFORMANCE

JEREMIAH CLARKE'S *Trumpet Voluntary* and Rossini's 'William Tell' Overture capture all the power of the trumpet to thrill. That same excitement is apparent in the grandeur of Louis Armstrong's 'West End Blues' and Dizzy Gillespie's exuberant 'Groovin' High', but compare the ethereal minimalism of Miles Davis's voice on *Sketches of Spain*. Leos Janácek deployed nine trumpets and two bass trumpets in his magnificent Sinfonietta.

CONNECTIONS

The **bass trumpet** was designed especially for use in Wagner's 'Ring' Cycle; the trombone now usually plays its low, mellow part. David Mason's **piccolo trumpet**, an octave above the standard, adds brilliance to The Beatles' 'Penny Lane'.

Tuba

IN ROMAN TIMES the word 'tuba' was applied to the trumpet, but now refers to the largest of the brass family. The tuba's tubby shape and association with the oom-pah band belies the instrument's potential to create a remarkably light and agile tone in the right hands: Gerard Hoffnung once remarked that when he was practising the tuba the neighbours thought he had an elephant trapped in his bathroom.

A relatively recent invention, first produced in Berlin in the 1820s, the tuba is rather like an outsize bugle or cornet, held upright with its bell pointing straight up. The wide conical bore produces a round, smooth sound which is moderated by anything from three to six valves.

The most frequently used of the tuba instruments is the F tuba, but close relations include:

- The euphonium: tenor tuba, mainstay of brass bands.
- The bass saxhorn: part of another, though less well known, integrated family of instruments invented by Adolphe Sax.
- Wagnerian tuba: a hybrid of tuba and French horn devised by the composer for use in his 'Ring' Cycle.

CLASSE D'OPHICLÉIDE
Cours des Minimes. — Section des Prodiges.

French caricature demonstrating the proportions of the ophicleide.

PERFORMANCE

VAUGHAN WILLIAMS wrote his Tuba Concerto at the age of 82: the first major concerto for the instrument, which had previously appeared in Wagner's *The Flying Dutchman* and Modest Mussorgsky's 'Bydlo' from *Pictures at an Exhibition*. Jazz outings include the tuba part for Bill Barber on 'Buzzard Song' from the Miles Davis/Gil Evans version of *Porgy and Bess*.

CONNECTIONS

The **tenor horn** is a much more slender version of the tuba, used in wind bands. The related **ophicleide**, looking like a metal bassoon, with keys not valves, was invented in the 1820s and widely played throughout the nineteenth century.

WOODWIND INSTRUMENTS
Introduction

THE WOODWINDS are one of the oldest families of instruments because of the very simple way in which they work. It is possible that the first 'wind' sounds were made when our earliest ancestors picked up hollow pieces of wood or shells and blew into them. This section covers the instruments in the woodwind family and key examples of other non-orchestral wind instruments. The name 'woodwind' is given, unsurprisingly, to those instruments that were originally made of wood (and mostly still are). These instruments fall into two main categories.

FLUTE

THE FLUTE TYPE can also be called an 'edge' instrument because the player blows towards a sharp edge, creating eddies that set the column of air vibrating – the flute and the recorder are examples. The principle is rather like blowing across the top of a bottle.

REED

ALL THE OTHER modern orchestral woodwind instruments employ reeds and there are two types of these: the single reed which is fixed on to the mouthpiece and made to vibrate when the player blows (e.g. a clarinet), and the double reed where the player blows to make the air vibrate between the two blades (e.g. an oboe).

In a typical modern orchestra at full size you might expect to find:

- Three flutes and a piccolo.
- Three oboes and a cor anglais.
- Three clarinets and a bass clarinet.
- Three bassoons and a double bassoon.

Bagpipe

SOMEWHERE, perhaps in Mesopotamia, about 7,000 years ago, a shepherd may well have looked at a goat skin and some hollow bones and had an idea for a new musical instrument: the bagpipe. In the early Christian era, the instrument spread from the Middle East eastward into India and westward to Europe. By the seventeenth century bagpipes were being played in European courts, but by the eighteenth century they were declining to become a minority folk instrument. In countries as diverse as Albania, Spain, Scotland and Ireland, the bagpipe is rightly valued as a living part of the culture.

PARTS OF A BAGPIPE

- Bag: the skin of a lamb or goat, made airtight, is squeezed using the arm or the knees to feed air to the chanter and drones.
- Blowpipe (or bellows): the player blows air into the bag through a single- or double-reeded pipe. Some designs supply air using a bellows instead.
- Chanter: a pipe with fingerholes that are covered to vary the melody. Some versions have a second chanter.
- Drones: the air leaves the bag through these reeded pipes to make a continuous drone. Three drones are common, two or one less so.

PERFORMANCE

HEAR SCOTTISH bagpipes swirl on the huge hit 'Mull of Kintyre' by Paul McCartney and Wings. Or you could buy the Mel Gibson video *Braveheart* to hear the sound of Uilleann piper Eric Riglersome on the soundtrack. Peter Maxwell Davies uses a piper to represent the sunrise in his entertaining *Orkney Wedding and Sunrise*.

CONNECTIONS

The bellows-blown **musette** was fashionable at the court of Louis XIV and was deployed by Jean-Philippe Rameau. In Brittany, the double-reed **bombard** is played in duet with a bagpipe.

Bagpiper in a marching band.

Bassoon

THE BASSOON is known for its twin characteristics – as the 'clown', for its comic effects, or the 'gentleman', for its eloquent, lyrical capacities. Its early development is thought to have followed the reconstruction of the shawm, a strident-sounding instrument often played in outdoor ceremonies during the Middle Ages and the Renaissance. Similarities in design and use also suggest the curtal or dulcian was the true forerunner of the bassoon.

It was used in Henry Purcell's 1691 score *The History of Dioclesian* and the English musicologist James Talbot identified 'a bassoon in four joynts' around 1695. The four-key version made by the Denners of Nuremberg was the eighteenth-century standard, and Carl Almenräder's 15-key bassoon met nineteenth-century demands for louder, more reliable, instruments. Two types now commonly used are made by the Heckel family and the Buffet-Crampon firm.

The bassoon has a smoother and less reedy sound than the oboe and is the true bass of the woodwind group. The size of this bass instrument poses special problems. The nine-foot-long tube has to be doubled back on itself and the finger-holes bored obliquely to be reached by the

Bassoons in the Philharmonic Orchestra.

player's fingers. Böhm's key innovations did not work well for the bassoon, and its resultant system is exceptionally difficult to play. With a reed made by bending double a shaped strip of cane, the bassoon's sound is one of the orchestra's primary colours.

PERFORMANCE

VIVALDI COMPLETED no fewer than 37 concertos for the bassoon, giving it both lyrical and jocular moods. The favourite depiction of the bassoon as a lumbering, pompous clown is surely in *The Sorcerer's Apprentice* by Paul Dukas. For a contrast, listen to the instrument's eerie opening to Stravinsky's *The Rite of Spring*.

CONNECTIONS

The nearest instrument is the **bass oboe** and various attempts have been made to build a satisfactory one. The **contrabassoon** sounds an octave lower than the bassoon.

Clarinet

THE CLARINET'S predecessor was a small single-reeded mock trumpet called a chalumeau. It is not certain, but th invention of the clarinet is ascribed to Johann Christoph Denner of Nuremburg in the early 1700s. With its strong upper register, it quickly found a place in military bands, but was not regularly used in the orchestra until around 1800. The clarinet is usually made of African blackwood. To play it, you blow, gripping the mouthpiece, reed down, between your lips or lower lip and upper teeth.

The clarinet has an acoustical feature that sets it apart: if yo blow harder, or 'overblow', on other woodwinds the pitch goes up an octave, but on a clarinet it goes up an octave and a fifth. The clarinet's separate registers produce a range of characteristi timbres (sounds) – rich and oily in the lowest register, slightly pale in the middle, clear and singing in the higher and rather shrill at the top.

There are two distinct key systems:

- Albert system: developed by Eugène Albert of Brussels, this is a modernisation of Iwan Müller's 13-key system of around 1812. Used in German-speaking countries.
- Böhm system: patented by Klosé and Buffet (Paris, 1844), it incorporates much of Böhm's 1832 flute fingering system. It brings many technical advantages and is standard in most countries.

PERFORMANCE

MOZART'S MARVELLOUS music for the clarinet – then a new instrument – includes his Quintet in A K581 and Concerto K622. The virtuosity of Benny Goodman, the undisputed 'King of Swing', can be heard on his 'Clarinet à la King'. And who can forget the insoucient ascending opening to George Gershwin's *Rhapsody in Blue*?

CONNECTIONS

As well as today's standard clarinet, the soprano in B flat, the instrument has taken varied forms, including: **clarinetto sestino**, **sopranino clarinet**, **basset horn** and **clarinette d'amour**.

Clarinet virtuoso Benny Goodman.

Didgeridoo

THIS IS PROBABLY the best-known instrument of Australia and is played by the Aboriginals of that country. At least 40 aboriginal names for it are known, from the north of Western Australia through the Arnhem Land peninsula to northern Queensland. Aboriginals trace the birth of the didgeridoo (also spelt didjeridu) to their ancestral Dreamtime, although some research

Didgeridoo playing at Glastonbury.

suggests its origin might have been as recent as 1,000 years ago.

A type of drone pipe or straight wooden trumpet, the didgeridoo is an unstopped hollowed piece of bamboo or wood about four or five feet long, with a bore of two inches or more and a mouth-piece made of wax or hardened gum. Bamboo didgeridoos are traditionally hollowed out with a fire stick or hot coals. The yidaki is a hardwood version particular to Arnhem Land. Although traditional instrument-making techniques continue, they have also been made out of salvaged materials such as exhaust pipes.

The player blows into the instrument trumpet-fashion; the sound can vary from a continuous fundamental drone to a sharp 'toot'. Using a process of circular breathing, with the cheeks being used much like bellows, players can set up remarkable continuous drones. Traditionally, the didgeridoo accompanies clicking sticks, singing and dancing, primarily in more 'open' ceremonies such as clan songs. Boys learn to play from an early age and talented players are recognised and held in high esteem by their community.

PERFORMANCE

ROLF HARRIS popularised the didgeridoo on his hit 'Sun Arise', but for authentic experience try 'Freedom' by Australia's leading aboriginal group, Yothu Yindi. Listen out for it in the jazz of McCoy Tyner's 'Uptown/Downtown', or combined with the Celtic sounds of The Chieftains on 'The Long Black Veil'.

CONNECTIONS

Similar, but found in a completely different setting, is the Alpine **alphorn**.

Flute

TO HAVE HEARD some of the earliest flute music, you would have had to be sitting in a cave 45,000 years ago, where a Neanderthal musician in Slovenia is thought to have fashioned such an instrument from the leg bone of a bear. The flute was known in ancient Greece by the second century BC, but it was not until around 1100 that it began to be used in Europe. King Henry VIII, a keen musician, had a good collection of them.

The sound is made when the flautist blows a stream of air against the edge of a hole in the side of the flute, causing the air enclosed in the instrument to vibrate. It was Theobald Böhm, a

Munich flute player and inventor, who made the modern instrument possible. His definitive 1847 design incorporated an ingenious system of keys and levers. Before keys, fingerholes had to be placed where the player could reach them; with keys they could be positioned to achieve the best possible note. A modern flute is made of wood, or more commonly (since the twentieth century) of metal such as silver; and it is 67 cm (26 ½ in) long.

Seventeenth-century 'nose-flute'.

PERFORMANCE

WHEN GENTLY played, the flute can be cool, even sensual – think of the languorous phrases in Debussy's *Prélude à l'après-midi d'un faune*. Two of Vivaldi's popular flute concertos have evocative titles: 'The Goldfinch' and 'The Stormy Sea'. Despite his supposed dislike of the instrument, Mozart's two flute concertos are among the most popular in his repertory.

CONNECTIONS

In addition to the concert flute in C, there are the **piccolo** (an octave higher), the **treble flute** in G (a fifth higher), the **alto flute** in G (a 4th lower) and the **bass flute** in C (an octave lower).

Kazoo

A KAZOO IS one of a family of instruments called mirlitons. They have in common a membrane which is vibrated by sound waves produced either by the player's voice or by an instrument. The distinctive sound produced has a buzzing quality, and the kazoo is the best-known member of the mirliton family. This has a membrane set into the wall of a short tube into which the player makes vocal noises. Many pop and jazz musicians have used kazoos in their music.

An even simpler homemade version has probably been tried by every child using tissue paper and a comb. Less well-known is the fact that certain flutes contain mirlitons, for example the Chinese ti, and that some African xylophones have mirliton resonators to give a slight rasping, rattling tone to the notes. Using the same principle, African mirlitons can even be found with a vibrating membrane made from spiders' webs.

PERFORMANCE

FOR SHEER zany fun it would be hard to beat the kazoo antics of the Bonzo Dog Doo-Dah Band on *The History of the Bonzos*. David Bedford wrote a piece called *With 101 Kazoos* for audience participation. Tchaikovsky's *Nutcracker Suite* includes a 'Dance of the Mirlitons', but this is usually interpreted as 'Reed-pipe Dance' and played on the flute.

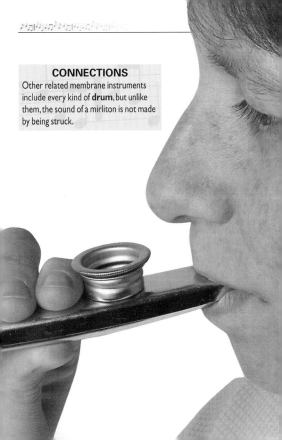

CONNECTIONS
Other related membrane instruments
include every kind of **drum**, but unlike
them, the sound of a mirliton is not made
by being struck.

Mouth Organ

THE ARRIVAL of the Chinese sheng in Europe in the eighteenth century encouraged a great deal of experimentation with free-reed instruments in the early nineteenth century. One of the most popular was produced by Friedrich Buschmann of Berlin in 1821; this was the *Mundäoline*, now known as the mouth organ or harmonica.

From the early twentieth century, the instrument was adopted by folk and blues musicians, particularly in the US. Blues players gave it the name 'harp' and could create powerful effects by altering the shape of the mouth, making the instrument shriek and moan or even imitate a rhythmic train.

Stevie Wonder.

Inside the mouth organ, free metal reeds are set in slots in a small, metal-enclosed wooden frame. The notes are sounded by alternately blowing and sucking through two parallel rows of wind channels. The reeds are positioned so that they respond to alternate directions of wind flow. The tongue covers channels not required. In chromatic (12-note scale) models, a finger-operated stop alternates between two sets of reeds tuned a semitone apart. They can range from two to four octaves in compass, and bass models are also played.

PERFORMANCE

THERE IS no mistaking the exuberant brilliance of Stevie Wonder's harmonica on *Songs in the Key of Life*. The jazz player Toots Thielemans performs his elegant quicksilver magic on Ella Fitzgerald's *Ella Abraca Jobim*. Sample the raw blues energy of Howlin' Wolf on his 'Smokestack Lightnin''.

CONNECTIONS

The **sheng** inspired a range of other free-reed instruments including the **harmonium**, the **concertina** and the **accordion**.

Oboe

THE WORD 'OBOE' comes from the French *hautbois*, meaning 'high (or loud) wood'. Its origins can be found in the shawm.

The orchestral oboe proper really came about during the mid-seventeenth century with the refinements of the French court musician, Jean Hotteterre, and others (it is worth noting that today, all orchestral instruments tune to the oboe). Having lost its former coarseness, it could be played indoors with stringed instruments and by the middle of the eighteenth century it was firmly established. Further improvements based on Theobald Böhm's key technologies have given the modern oboe one of the most complex key systems. The main types of oboe are:

Eighteenth-century musician playing a hautbois.

- Treble or soprano oboe: the principal member of the family, pitched in C.

- Oboe d'amore : the alto oboe, pitched in A. So called for the warmth of its sound and much used in J. S. Bach's time.
- Cor anglais or English horn: neither English nor a horn, it is a tenor oboe pitched in F with a richer, more throaty tone.
- Baritone oboe: possibly originating in the seventeenth century, this is pitched in C an octave below the soprano.

If you're an oboe player, your life revolves around your reeds, made from the bamboo-like plant *Arundo donax*. Most serious players make their own, although ready made reeds can be bought.

PERFORMANCE

BACH USED the oboe d'amore in 60 works, notably the *St John Passion*. The oboe also makes an impression in Debussy's *Images* and is stirring in Ravel's *Boléro*. One of the most poignant solos for cor anglais is in Dvorák's Symphony No. 9.

CONNECTIONS

Double-reed instruments related to the oboe occur in many cultures around the world, for example the North African **zurna** and the Indian **shahnai**. Wilhelm Heckel's **heckelphone** (1904) is a low-register combination of oboe and alphorn.

Panpipes

ACCORDING TO Greek legend, when Pan pursued the mountain-nymph Syrinx to the river's edge, she was transformed into reeds which he then fashioned into the Pan's pipes or Syrinx. The panpipes was also known in many other parts of the world, including China, Egypt and Oceania. In parts of Europe, for example the Pyrénées, it has been mainly a shepherd's instrument. In Romania, by contrast, the 15- to 29-pipe instrument called a nai is played in virtuoso professional folk groups. Panpipes are at their most haunting when heard in South American folk ensembles, whose melodies evoke the mystery and atmosphere of snow-capped mountains. They are still popular in many parts of that continent, such as Chile, Argentina, Bolivia, Paraguay and Peru.

The panpipes is a wind instrument consisting of cane pipes of different lengths, tied in a row or held together by other means and generally closed at the bottom. Metal, clay or wood

Panpipes from South America.

versions are also made. The sound is produced when the player holds the pipe end to their mouth, blowing across the hole. Each pipe gives a different note. Although usually hand-held, the largest of the South American siku can exceed 2 m (6.5 ft) and has to be rested on the ground.

PERFORMANCE

GEORG PHILIPP TELEMANN wrote a short piece called *Flauto Pastorale* for syrinx in 1721. The many compositions of the Romanian virtuoso Gheorghe Zamfir include a Concerto and a Rhapsody. The group Waykis evoke the sound of the Andes on their 'Inca Gold'.

CONNECTIONS

In South America, panpipes are often played in conjunction with a large drum called a **bomba**.

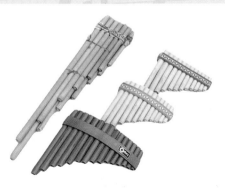

Piccolo

T HIS INSTRUMENT'S full name – *Flauto Piccolo*, Italian for 'small flute' – says it all. It is the highest-pitched woodwind instrument to be found in orchestras and military bands, and its orchestral use dates from around the end of the eighteenth century, when it replaced the flageolet (also called at that time 'flauto piccolo'). As with the flute, the player holds the instrument sideways and blows across the edge of a hole in the side of the instrument, finding just the right angle to make the sound. The sound has a high-pitched and shrill quality and can be heard above the range of other orchestral instruments.

Half the size of the standard flute, the piccolo has a conical or cylindrical bore and is a transverse (horizontally played) instrument. As with the ordinary concert flute, it is fitted with a key system developed by Theobald Böhm and the fingering is exactly the same. To make it easier for players of both instruments, piccolo music is written so that it looks the same, but the notes produced by a piccolo are actually an octave higher than as written on the page.

PERFORMANCE

BEETHOVEN WAS one of the first composers to use the piccolo, and you won't hear a finer example of its orchestral

effect than the high answering flourishes above the combined might of a full orchestra near the thrilling climax of his Fifth Symphony. Over a century later, the piccolo's shrill coldness contributed much to the chilly symphonic domain of Dmitri Shostakovich.

The piccolo is played transversely.

CONNECTIONS

A six-keyed version in the key of D was formerly used in military bands so that it could play in flat keys. The piccolo is also closely linked to the shrill-toned **fife**, which dates from twelfth-century Europe and has been played with drums to accompany marching infantry since the time of the Crusades.

Recorder

THE RECORDER has a long history in Western music, probably dating back to the fourteenth century, when it appears to have been a development from an earlier kindred instrument. In 1619 Michael Praetorius listed seven members of the recorder family in his *Syntagmatis Musici Tomus Secundus*. Its chief repertory comes from the Renaissance and Baroque periods, when it was very popular. Many composers, including J. S. Bach and George Frideric Handel, included recorder parts in their works, but its clear piping sound

Recorders come in different sizes, offering a variety of ranges.

fell out of favour during the late eighteenth century.

The recorder was revived in 1919 by the English instrument maker Arnold Dolmetsch. Since this time the design of recorders has followed the early eighteenth-century Baroque style. They are made in four main sizes: descant (or soprano), treble (or alto), tenor and bass, although great bass, double bass and sporanino instruments are also made. They are traditionally made of wood, occasionally of ivory, although thousands are now made for schools using plastic.

The recorder has a beak-like mouthpiece at the top end of the instrument with a whistle-like aperture that provides the edge that makes the air vibrate when blown. The cylindrical body has holes that can be covered by seven fingers at the front and one thumb at the back to make different notes.

PERFORMANCE

YOU MAY be able to pick out the recorder parts in some medieval compositions, but perhaps the most engaging recorder music can be found at the next local school concert, especially if someone you know is playing.

CONNECTIONS

The recorder is closely related to the **flageolet**. It is also linked to the **flute**; in Vivaldi's day, the **treble recorder** was known as the 'common flute'.

World of Wind

P EOPLE HAVE probably been blowing into things to make
  sounds since the beginning of time. Here is a selection of
some of the perhaps less well-known 'blown' instruments
around the world.

- Alphorn: first made from a hollowed tree trunk, this long
  horn is famous for its cow-like signalling sound that carries
  for miles over the Alps.
- Aulos: Mediterranean folk players need strong cheeks
  and lungs to play this double-reed instrument with one
  to three pipes.
- Conch shell: originally blown to frighten enemies; the
  ancient conch shell trumpet is still played in ceremonies
  from Polynesia to Mexico.
- Ocarina: this elongated egg-shaped instrument was
  originally made from baked mud and, later, terracotta.
- Ophicleide: invented in France in 1821 as an improvement
  on the serpent, it was itself replaced by the bass
  tuba in orchestras.
- Palawta: variations on this six-hole flute are played in
  the Philippines. It is played transverse as is the modern
  Western flute.
- Putu (or Pututu): the indigenous people of the Atacamá
  desert region of Chile play this natural horn to accompany
  ancient rituals.
- Serpent: invented in sixteenth-century France, this is a long
  wooden tube shaped in a double 'S'.
- Shahnai: a two-reed oboe or shawm with a small flared bell

and a very piercing sound. It is played in northern India, Bangladesh and Persia.

- Shofar: a ram's-horn trumpet, mainly used at important Jewish public and religious occasions.
- Trutruka: a strange-looking combination of vegetable-stem trumpet with an animal horn sticking out at a right angle, found in Chile and Argentina.

Composer John Cage wrote for the unusual instrument, the conch shell.

STRINGED INSTRUMENTS

Introduction

THE STRINGED instruments that we are most familiar with – the violins, violas, cellos and double basses which form the orchestral string section, and the acoustic guitar – have changed remarkably little since the 1600s, when their long evolution came to fruition.

To produce their sound, stringed instruments fall into two main categories:

- Plucked: with the fingers, fingernails, pick or plectrum, e.g. harp, mandolin, sitar.
- Bowed: with a length of horsehair (or a similar material) brushing against the strings, e.g. viol, double bass.

There is also a small group of instruments - the dulcimer, for example – where the strings are hit by hammers or beaters. We have included, too, the aeolian harp, which is played by the natural force of the wind.

The combination of orchestral stringed instruments has long had a major influence on the history of chamber music: just listen to Mozart's String Trio In E Flat Major or Franz Schubert's Trout Quintet. Samuel Barber's Adagio for Strings also displays their strong emotional pull – the ability, appropriately, to tug at our heartstrings. In the last few decades, other arrangers and musicians have realised the potential: the brilliant decision to add pizzicato strings to Buddy Holly's 'Raining in my Heart', the ever

experimental George Martin's use of a string quartet on The Beatles' 'Eleanor Rigby', and Björk's Talvin Singh-arranged string backing on her *Debut* album.

In general, the plucked stringed instruments have tended to be used either for solo performance or in an accompanying role – although Russian balalaika orchestras, guitar orchestras and mandolin ensembles have all existed.

Acoustic Guitar

THROUGHOUT ITS HISTORY, the guitar has – perhaps more than any other instrument – managed to bridge the gap between the often disconnected worlds of classical, folk and popular music. Its roots go back to Babylonian times, when reliefs reveal a plucked, guitar-like instrument; by the 1500s it was prevalent in Spain, and is still sometimes called the Spanish guitar.

Medieval versions – like the lute – sometimes sported rounded backs and paired strings: the 12-string guitar still exists (its ringing tone stands out

Elvis Presley's D-18 Martin acoustic guitar.

on the Byrds' 'Mr Tambourine Man'). The standardised modern acoustic guitar has a flat back and sound board with a pronounced curved 'waist' to the body.

The acoustic guitar remained relatively unchanged until the twentieth century, when additions included steel strings for greater attack in dance-band settings, where it took over from the banjo. This marked the beginning of the guitar's rise to a major role in popular music, leading directly to the development of the semi-acoustic and fully electric versions (see p. 150).

PERFORMANCE

RODRIGO'S *Concierto de Aranjuez* is one of the best-known examples of the acoustic guitar in a classical setting; Heitor Villa-Lobos's Concerto for Guitar and Small Orchestra demands a virtuoso performance. The guitar is equally as comfortable in folk/blues settings (Blind Lemon Jefferson's 'Tin Cup Blues'), jazz (Django Reinhardt on 'Lady Be Good'), the pop song (Simon and Garfunkel's 'Mrs Robinson') or even in the heavy metal world (Extreme's 'More Than Words').

CONNECTIONS

The **vihuela** was a flat-backed plucked instrument popular in the sixteenth century, superseded by the guitar. The **dobro steel resonator guitar**, invented by the Dopera brothers in California in the 1920s, was designed to provide extra volume.

Aeolian Harp

THE AEOLIAN HARP is one of the rare instruments that does not require a human player. Even more significantly, there is no automatic or mechanical replacement for the performer, as there is in the player piano, for example. All that the aeolian harp requires is the wind to activate its otherworldly sound – it takes its name from Aeolus, the Greek god of the winds.

The harp's origins are somewhat obscure, although it was certainly in use from the end of the sixteenth century. In construction it is not unlike the dulcimer: a box-like rectangular frame, about a metre long, with a range of strings made of gut laid across it. Each of these strings is tuned in unison (in other words, all to the same note) and the instrument is positioned at a suitable location to catch the wind. The current of air vibrates the strings to produce a soft humming sound; the stronger the wind the more harmonic overtones come into play, creating disembodied chords.

There have been efforts to modify the simplicity of the harp by tuning the strings to a chord, but it is generally accepted that the purest form is the best. Some organs attempt to imitate its soft sound with a stop called the Aeolina or Aeoline.

PERFORMANCE

THERE ARE FEW recorded examples of the aeolian harp, but Norwegian saxophonist Jan Garbarek carried out an interesting exercise on the album *Dis* when he interacted with an unmanned wind harp and the North Sea winds on the track 'Vandrere'.

CONNECTIONS

Another instrument which relies on the forces of nature to produce its sound are the tinkling **wind chimes**.

Balalaika

T HE TRIANGULAR SHAPE of the balalaika is universally recognised, but few people are aware of the importance of its role in Eastern European music; the balalaika is the Russian guitar. Lute-like predecessors were known from as early as the twelfth century, but it was a Russian nobleman called Vasily Andreyev, a virtuoso balalaika performer, who improved, modified and standardised the traditional instrument in the late 1800s.

Andreyev's basic balalaika is characterised by the familiar shape: three strings and a fretted neck. The most common version is the 'prima balalaika', which unusually has two of the three strings tuned to the same note: despite this apparent restriction the instrument has a surprisingly large range. In addition the top two strings are set much closer together, allowing the bottom string to be plucked hard by the left-hand thumb, creating the typical strumming effect.

Another of Andreyev's innovations was the creation of a balalaika family in a choice of sizes – from piccolo to contrabass. This range means that entire balalaika orchestras can be created using the one instrument, often backed up by the bayan (a Russian accordion), tambourines and various flutes and pipes.

PERFORMANCE

ANYONE WHO has seen the film *Dr Zhivago* will be aware of the traditional balalaika sound used in 'Lara's Theme'. Classical composers have responded to its sound, notably Yuri Shushakov's 1955 Balalaika Concerto. In some salsa line-ups the related tres can be heard in action, for example on the Fania All Stars' 'Soy Guajiro'.

The balalaika family.

CONNECTIONS

The balalaika is most closely linked to the **lute**, but the **tres**, a Latin American three-stringed guitar, has many of the same qualities.

Banjo

I N 1688 THE physician and naturalist Hans Sloane came across an instrument in Jamaica which he noted down as the 'strum-strum'. This was probably an early banjo, which had come to the Americas along with the shiploads of slaves transported from north-west Africa.

The banjo's most distinguishing features are its circular vellum or skin – a bit like a snare drum head – and long neck; a standard issue banjo has five strings, usually made of steel, although any number from four to nine are known. One string carries the melody, while the rest are ripe for finger-picking. The instrument's dry tone has a percussive penetrating power and so it proved useful in adding volume and crispness in unamplified bands.

After the banjo's arrival in the New World, it accompanied spirituals, and thence became a regular ingredient in the Black Minstrel (and white pseudo-Minstrel) movement. In turn this led to its involvement in traditional Dixieland jazz; in the 1940s

Bill Monroe
introduced it to
bluegrass music, from
where it found its way
into the 1970s country
rock sound. The banjo
also features in the
music of countries as
distant as Malawi and
Morocco.

PERFORMANCE

EARL SCRUGGS,
one of Bill Monroe's
original Bluegrass Boys,
added his lick-driven
'Foggy Mountain
Breakdown' to a car
chase on the sound-
track of *Bonnie and
Clyde*. Also listen to the famous banjo

Gypsy banjo player.

duet in the film *Deliverance* or Doug Dillard playing on 'Banjo
in the Hollow'. Gershwin's *Porgy and Bess* includes the banjo on
'I Got Plenty O' Nuttin'', while Bela Fleck creates the closest
thing to be-bop banjo on his album *Flight of the Cosmic Hippo*.

CONNECTIONS

The **ngoni**, a traditional rectangular **lute** with a vellum sounding board,
found in the music of Mali and Guinea, may have been the origin of
the banjo.

Cello

THROUGH PERFORMERS like Jacqueline du Pré and Paul Tortelier, the cello has created a position for itself within the orchestral string family as an emotional vehicle, less brilliant and showy than the violin, less mysterious than the viola, more heart-rending than the double bass.

The full name of the cello is 'violoncello', a small violone or bass viol. However its original name 'basso di viola di braccio' meaning 'bass arm viol' suggest that its roots lie more closely with the violin. The current tuning and size of the cello were pretty well fixed by the end of the seventeenth century, and the instrument established itself through continuous work in the Baroque period, asserting dominance over its closest challenger, the bass viol.

Surprisingly, despite its expressiveness, which appealed greatly to the Romantic movement, solo cello works were relatively infrequent until the arrival of the great soloists of the twentieth century –

such as Pablo Casals and Yo Yo Ma – encouraged a cluster of works from the likes of Edward Elgar and Shostakovich. By contrast, Brazilian composer Villa-Lobos uses eight cellos and no other instruments to support a soprano voice in his 'Cantilena' from *Bachianas Brasilieras No. 5*.

PERFORMANCE

THE SLOW MOVEMENT of Johannes Brahms' Piano Concerto No. 2 includes a solo cello theme considered bold by his contemporaries; both Elgar's and Dvorák's Cello Concertos have great emotional depth; and the Swan theme from Saint-Saëns' *Carnival of the Animals* is pure melody. The Electric Light Orchestra introduced the rock cello on 'Roll Over Beethoven'.

CONNECTIONS

The **sarangi** used in classical Indian music is also bowed and played upright, but players use their nails rather than fingertips to stop the strings.

Left: Jacqueline du Pré.

Double Bass

THE DOUBLE BASS was for a long time no more than a reinforcement at the foot of orchestral string arrangements, often merely echoing the cello part. It was rarely given a chance to shine by classical composers, but thanks to jazz the double bass found its voice with a vengeance, and was free to come out of the twilight into the limelight – even helping to kick off rock'n'roll on early Elvis tracks like 'That's All Right (Mama)'.

Of all the orchestral string instruments, the double bass is the most closely related to the viol, as a direct descendant of the sixteenth-century violone – a heritage revealed in its steeply sloping shoulders. The bass viol carried six strings; over time the number of strings dropped to four, although some modern double basses have a fifth string for

Bassist Charles Mingus.

rumbling low work. The double bass is available in a number of sizes: for orchestral work the three-quarter size is more common than the awkward full-size version.

Lower metal strings on the bass are not far off the consistency of steel hawsers, and bass players' fingers are usually topped off by a fine range of calluses. In jazz settings the bass is generally plucked rather than bowed, whereas in orchestral settings it is the other way around. Jazz players are sometimes amplified to compete with the volume of the other instruments.

PERFORMANCE

MAHLER'S SYMPHONY No. 1 gives the double basses a minor theme to 'Frère Jacques'; Saint-Saëns let them enjoy themselves imitating elephants in *Carnival of the Animals*. Jazz bassist Charles Mingus is dynamic on his 1959 'Wednesday Night Prayer Meeting'; Charlie Haden duets meditatively with guitarist Pat Metheny on the album *Beyond the Missouri Sky*.

CONNECTIONS

The **violone**, or bass viol, outmoded by the double bass, has been rediscovered as part of the authentic music revival.

Harp

THE HARP is an instrument of great antiquity, appearing with frequency in the art and literature of the ancient Egyptians, Greeks, Hebrews and Celts – and during the medieval period. Common to all are an open frame, either curved or a two-sided angle – later enclosed by a fore-pillar – which contains strings vibrated by plucking.

The orchestral harp dates from the 1840s, a complex (and expensive) development of the simple frame harp. Expanding its range has been a challenge throughout its history, since all the strings are tuned to just one major scale – C flat major on today's harp. Awkward systems of hooks were tried out before a pedal system was developed in Bavaria and France. Seven pedals and a pin mechanism take the pitch of one set of strings up a semitone or tone.

Egyptian priests playing the harp.

The most commonly used harp techniques are the arpeggio – the notes of a chord rippled quickly and successively – and the glissando, the sweeping up and down of the strings that has unfortunately become a musical cliché. Harpists can in fact

perform music as complex as that for the piano, although they can only play eight rather than 10 notes at one time, since the little finger is not used.

PERFORMANCE

ONE OF THE best-known harp pieces is the introduction to the 'Waltz of the Flowers' in Tchaikovsky's *Nutcracker Suite*; Benjamin Britten's interlude in *A Ceremony of Carols* is spare and wintery. Gabriel Fauré's Impromptu Opus 86 shows off a wide range of techniques. The harp's seductive washes of colour were marvellously deployed after the First World War, such as in Ravel's *Daphnis and Chloë*.

CONNECTIONS

The **clàrsach** is a small Celtic harp. An orchestral player would call this pedal harp a 'telyn'. The **lyre** and **kithara** are close relatives of the harp.

Lute

A STRONG VISUAL reminder of medieval music, the lute was a predominant instrument between the fifteenth and seventeenth centuries. However, it eventually lost out to the guitar as the most used of the portable plucked instruments: the guitar proved more brilliant and more versatile, but the musical world was deprived of the shimmering subtlety and persuasive charm that had made lutenists hypnotic performers.

Probably of Middle Eastern origin, derived from the Arab 'ud (which is still in use today), the lute gained wide coverage in Europe, from the French luth to the Romanian quitara – it was this European version that sported the body shape of a pear sliced in half. Other elements which set it apart from the guitar included the lack of a bridge, an ornate rose soundhole and the peg-box head at the top of the neck.

The lute contained a number of variations on the theme, including the large, double-necked arch-lute and the longer-necked theorbo.

Lute music was not read from classical musical notation but employed 'tablature', a graphic representation that indicated the frets to be used. Within the music, the lute player – plucking with his or her

Renaissance lutenist, flautist and singer.

fingers and in direct touch with the strings – had room to explore beautiful, gentle improvisations, either as a solo performer or accompanying dance or song.

PERFORMANCE

JOHN DOWLAND'S *My Thoughts are Wing'd with Hopes* is just one of his extensive output of solo lute pieces; his *Lachrimae* (or *Seven Teares*) is a mournful lament. Baroque compositions include David Kellner's Fantasia in C Minor and J. S. Bach's Suite for Lute in G Minor.

CONNECTIONS

Lute-like instruments appear in many cultures – including the Egyptian **gurumi**, the Indian **tambura** and the Japanese **shamisen**.

Mandolin

THE MANDOLIN has some of the aspects of the guitar, violin and the lute – but unlike the lute it experienced a revival in the twentieth century in country and bluegrass.

The mandolin received an unexpected boost in public awareness thanks to the best-selling novel *Captain Corelli's Mandolin* by Louis de Bernières, himself a mandolin enthusiast. The instrument's name, derived from the Italian diminutive for an almond, refers to the shape of its body, which is often constructed from rosewood and inlaid with tortoiseshell.

Descended from the mandola, a fifteenth-century lute, the mandolin, or mandoline, has frets and a bridge like a guitar, but its strings are set in pairs tuned to the same note. The main

technique involves playing these with a rapid
tremolo, using a plectrum, to achieve a strongly
percussive sound. Given the instrument's
relatively small size, great dexterity is also
required because the frets are so close to
one another.

*Eighteenth-
century
mandolin
and its case.*

The mandolin has long been a
popular instrument in southern
Italy for serenaders – in Mozart's
Don Giovanni, the Don
serenades Elvira's maid on the
mandolin in 'Deh, vieni alla
finestra' – and featured in
mandolin orchestras through to the beginning of
the twentieth century. Bill Monroe, the father
of bluegrass music, gave it another lease of
life when he introduced the instrument to
American country music in the 1940s.

PERFORMANCE

THE MANDOLIN makes a few appearances in classical
music: Vivaldi wrote a Concerto For Two Mandolins, while a
more unusual occurrence is in the third movement of Mahler's
Symphony No. 7. The Eagles' Bernie Leadon adds his
mandolin skills to their 'Hollywood Waltz'. Mandolin master
David 'Dawg' Grisman guested on the Grateful Dead's 'Ripple'.

CONNECTIONS

The long-necked **bouzouki** from Greece also relies on the tremolo
technique – its sound best known from the film *Zorba the Greek*.

Sitar

TO WESTERN EARS the sitar became the quintessential sound of Indian music following its somewhat faddish promotion by The Beatles (through their collaboration with Ravi Shankar), The Rolling Stones and Traffic in the late 1960s – though its haunting sound has been a central part of Indian classical music for centuries.

Developed in the thirteenth century, the bulb-like body of the sitar, with something of the lute about it, is balanced by a thick fingerboard and extended neck. There are two sets of strings: four strings which play the melody line along with two or three drones, and a separate group of a dozen or more 'sympathetic' strings which resonate in performance. A set of brass frets are both movable and curved, producing the instrument's distinctive bending, portamento sound.

Ravi Shankar.

Played in the lotus position, the sitar forms part of the classical Indian group, including the tabla, sarangi (a cello-like instrument) and shahnai (a relation of the oboe). Together they work around the complex improvised patterns of the raga, still alien to Western audiences: at the Concert for Bangladesh in 1971, Ravi Shankar received a rapturous ovation after several minutes, only to explain that he had in fact just been tuning up.

PERFORMANCE
GEORGE HARRISON played sitar on 'Norwegian Wood', Brian Jones followed suit on 'Paint it Black'. By contrast, Ananda Shankar, nephew of Ravi, created a crossover version of the Doors' 'Light My Fire'. An electric sitar, which helps guitarists approximate the authentic sound, is used by Steely Dan's Denny Dias on 'Do it Again'.

CONNECTIONS
The **dilruba** is a smaller version of the sitar, played with a bow; the **surbahar** is effectively a bass sitar.

Ukulele

THE UKULELE, identified so closely with Hawaii, arrived on the island literally out of the blue, on a boat that arrived in Honolulu one day in 1879. One of the passengers produced a 'braguinha' (a small Portuguese guitar) and the locals were smitten, adopting the instrument and calling it after a Polynesian word for a jumping flea – maybe referring to the movements of the player's fingers.

The tiny body of the braguinha was slightly enlarged – though not by much – and was strung with gut rather than steel. The native koa, an acacia, provided wood for the body. The versatile, and portable, ukulele was promoted by the Hawaiian royal family (one of whom wrote the classic 'Aloha Oe'), and then unleashed in the US after Hawaii took a stand at a San Francisco exposition in 1915. As things from the South Pacific came

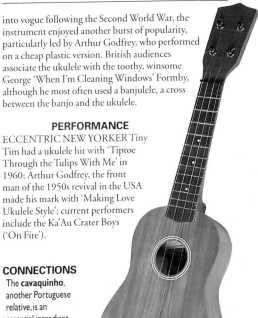

into vogue following the Second World War, the instrument enjoyed another burst of popularity, particularly led by Arthur Godfrey, who performed on a cheap plastic version. British audiences associate the ukulele with the toothy, winsome George 'When I'm Cleaning Windows' Formby, although he most often used a banjulele, a cross between the banjo and the ukulele.

PERFORMANCE

ECCENTRIC NEW YORKER Tiny Tim had a ukulele hit with 'Tiptoe Through the Tulips With Me' in 1960; Arthur Godfrey, the front man of the 1950s revival in the USA made his mark with 'Making Love Ukulele Style'; current performers include the Ka'Au Crater Boys ('On Fire').

CONNECTIONS

The **cavaquinho**, another Portuguese relative, is an essential ingredient in the morna music of the Cape Verde islands.

Viol

PARTLY BECAUSE of the similarity of the names involved, viols are often assumed to be a variation of the orchestral string family. In fact, the viol family is a completely separate range of instruments (and indeed the first of the two to develop a distinctive identity) which were among the most important in Renaissance and early Baroque music.

The significant characteristics of the viol family, which probably originated in North Africa and reached Europe via Spain, are their completely flat back, sloping shoulders and fretted neck. Most viols have six gut strings – difficult to tune – and were always played in an upright position gripped between the knees.

The viol was particularly popular in England and France in the 1600s – households might own a chest of viols in different sizes, from treble to bass, and whole families played together. Charles I had his own consort, as did Oliver Cromwell.

However the viol had effectively disappeared by the time the classical orchestra was established, and it was only in the 1890s that the instrument maker Arnold Dolmetsch promoted its revival.

Sixteenth-century viol player.

PERFORMANCE

FIVE VIOLS are required for the 1599 pavan *The Countess of Pembroke's Funerall*, by Antony Holborne; Purcell's *Complete Fantasias* proved to be one of the last important works for the Renaissance viol. Marin Marais' *Pièces de Viole* are fine examples of the French school of viol music; J. S. Bach's *Sonata in G Minor* is a Baroque masterpiece. The 1992 film *Tous les Matins du Monde* tells the life-story of seventeenth-century violists Saint-Colombe and Marais and includes many of their original compositions.

CONNECTIONS

The **viola d'amore**, of which Vivaldi was a fan, had the same back and shoulders as a viol but no frets, was played on the shoulder like a viola and sported sympathetic resonating strings.

Viola

THE VIOLA has been described as the Cinderella of the string section, frequently ignored and derided as something of a makeweight. However, its rich, mellow sound is a treat for the cognoscenti, who appreciate its value as a gastronome might savour a particularly exquisite truffle – indeed, woody and nutty are adjectives often applied to its tone.

Of all the strings, it is the one that bears the Italian name for the whole family – but by the end of the sixteenth century it had specifically come to mean the alto partner of the violin, tuned a fifth below its showier cousin. To correspond to that drop in pitch, it should be half as long again as the violin, making playing under the chin impractical; a compromise

was reached, but even so the size of the instrument makes it difficult to hold.

Just as the double bass originally tended to echo the cello line, the viola had much the same role, shadowing the violins or even the bass; there are still few concertos or sonatas for the viola – which is something of a shame when you learn that many great composers were violists, including Mozart and J. S. Bach.

PERFORMANCE

THE UNFINISHED Béla Bartók Viola Concerto was championed by Yehudi Menuhin; Berlioz's viola solo from *Harold in Italy* was commissioned by Nicolo Paganini, who in the end never performed it himself. Vaughan Williams also gave the viola a fine solo in his suite *Flos Campi* (known to irreverent musicians as 'Camp Flossie').

CONNECTIONS

The **viola alta** was a full-sized, five-stringed viola introduced in the 1870s, constructed in proportion to its pitch and extremely arduous to play.

Violin

THE VIOLIN is perhaps the most familiar part of the classical orchestra and it is surprising that despite the scrolled head and horsehair bow that hark back to ages past, it i still the dominant orchestral instrument as well as a major force in folk, county and ethnic music.

Although there have been modifications to the instrument over the centuries, the violin of the 1600s is to all intents and purposes the same used today, including the f-shaped sound holes, the polished body with separate front and back, and the wooden tuning pegs. A straight and adjustable bow, the use of metal strings and the addition of a chin-rest were all in place by the nineteenth century.

Virtuosos such as Paganini could delight in the violin's instant and agile response and exploit its armoury of techniques, including pronounced vibrato, staccato and

The great violinist Yehudi Menuhin.

pizzicato and more arcane techniques like striking the strings
with the wood of the bow ('con legno') or bowing tight up to
the bridge to create a deliberately harsher tone ('sul ponticello').

PERFORMANCE

THE GREAT violin concertos include the Brahms D Major
and Felix Mendelssohn's No. 2 in E Minor; Nicolai Rimsky-
Korsakov's *Sheherazade* uses the solo violin to voice the role of
the work's alluring narrator. Paganini's *Caprices* and Bach's D-
Minor Partita (both for solo violin) remain a challenge to all but
the most gifted. A lack of formal restraint is nonchalantly
displayed in jazz violin by Stephane Grappelli on 'I Got
Rhythm' and in the Celtic idiom by Máire Breatnach on the
soundtrack to *Riverdance*.

CONNECTIONS

The **fiedel** – a medieval precursor of
both violins and viols – is the origin of the
violin's nickname of 'fiddle'.

*Stephane
Grappelli.*

Classic Violin Makes

I N ONE SMALL CORNER of Italy – the Lombardy town of
Cremona – three families dominated the world of violin
manufacture for the best part of two hundred years: Amati,
Guarneri and Stradivari. Their craftsmanship lives on, since the
finest examples of their work have become iconic, highly
collectable and extremely expensive items, much sought after
by leading violinists.

- The earliest of these dynasties of violin makers were the
  Amati, founded by Andrea Amati, whose first known
  instrument is dated 1564. His two sons and his brother
  continued the tradition, but it was his grandson Niccolò
  who garnered the most fame, and passed on the heritage of
  his family's skills to both Andreas Guarneri and Antonio
  Stradivari. Amati violins set a benchmark for the shape of
  the violin, and are noted for their delicacy and elegance,
  perfect for chamber music.

Eighteenth-century violin by
Andreas Guarneri's son, Pietro.

- Andreas Guarneri also had two sons and a grandson to develop the Guarneri legacy; and again it was the grandson, Giuseppe Antonio Amati (1698–1744), who was the most highly regarded – he was known as Giuseppe del Gesù, since his signature on each completed violin was rounded off with the letters IHS (the Greek abbreviation for Jesus). Eschewing precise craftsmanship, all the Guarneri violins were highly individual, giving each a distinct personality.

- It was Antonio Stradivari (1644–1737), better known by the Latin form of his name, 'Stradivarius', who developed the Cremona violin to the version many players consider most perfect – adding power and brilliance to impeccable design standards. Stradivarius's sons followed him into the business but they were unable to match the talent of their father, who created some 1,000 instruments – including violas and cellos – over 70 years of work.

Zither

T HE ZITHER is part of a group of instruments which are linked by the fact that sets of strings run parallel to their main body, and that – unlike, say, the lute, lyre or harp – they can still be played even without the presence of a resonating device. In the concept's least advanced state, native instruments exist which are little more than a stick carrying strings along its length.

Closely identified with the Alpine region of Europe – and particularly the Austrian Tyrol – the zither is a closed wooden box which has anything from 30 to 40 strings lying across its surface. A number of these strings are placed over frets and can be stopped by the thumb of

The zither in an Austrian band.

the left hand, while the right plucks the strings with a plectrum to pick out melodies or chords. In performance, the zither is usually placed on a table or on the knees of the performer.

Because the construction of the zither resembles keyboard instruments such as the harpsichord, it is sometimes seen as a relative of theirs. Other variants include:

- The dulcimer: struck by small wooden beaters, and popular in Hungarian and Romanian folk music.
- The cimbalom: a concert version of the dulcimer used for orchestral purposes.

PERFORMANCE

THE 'HARRY LIME THEME', written by Anton Karas for the film *The Third Man*, is a haunting piece of zither music; Johann Strauss added its colour to *Tales from the Vienna Woods*. The cimbalom is requested in Stravinsky's *Rag-Time*, and also features memorably in Zoltán Kodály's folk-based *Janos* suite.

CONNECTIONS

The **psaltery**, an instrument used in the twelfth to fifteenth centuries, the **vina** of Indian classical music and the 13-stringed **koto** of Japan are all based on the same principles as the zither.

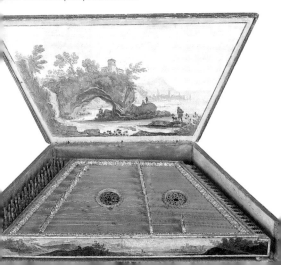

KEYBOARD INSTRUMENTS

Introduction

INSTRUMENTS WITH keyboards allow the performer to control the sound they produce by some kind of mechanical process – that rather technical description does not, of course, explain the genius that a human player can add. In fact, it is the interaction between the creativity of the player and the engineering at his or her disposal that make keyboards so fascinating.

There are two principal categories of instruments:

- Touch sensitive: where pressure on the key directly affects the sound quality of the note produced, e.g. piano, clavichord.

- Non-sensitive: where the key simply triggers a separate process, e.g. organ, harpsichord.

Nearly all allow the use of both hands (and feet, on the organ) to provide maximum coverage – sometimes even 10 fingers seem not quite enough!

We are all now used to the centuries-old arrangement of white and black keys. It was not always so. On the organs of the second millennium AD and earlier, there was simply a set of broad keys – some so wide they had to be depressed with a clenched fist – to produce the seven notes of the plainsong mode then in use. But with the arrival of 'musica ficta' (feigned music), sharpened or flattened notes were required: the first to appear was B flat, neatly tucked between the A and B notes.

Gradually the other four short, narrow keys were added, and there the keyboard has stayed ever since. Attempts to come up with alternative, more efficient methods have been tried, but none have come close to catching on. The keyboard arrangement we know, like that of the typewriter's QWERTY layout, just is and probably always will be.

Clavichord

THE CLAVICHORD affirms its place as the earliest of the string keyboard instruments in its very name, taken from the Latin for, simply, key and string. Chronologically older than the virginal and spinet – it is first mentioned in the 1400s – the clavichord differs from both since its strings were not plucked, and from the piano because they were not hit by hammers. Instead, small brass blades known as tangents would strike the strings from underneath.

The tangent would lift, strike and then hold the string in position, acting like a guitarist's or violinist's finger to determine the length of the vibrating string. This lessened the power of the instrument. However, what the clavichord lacked in volume it made up for in its response to the player's touch: the harder the key was pressed, the louder the note. After striking the string the player could also move the key up and down while the string continued to vibrate, creating a vibrato effect called 'bebung'.

Seventeenth-century illustration showing a clavichord.

Co-existing with the harpsichord from the sixteenth century onwards, the clavichord was popular for solo recitals throughout Europe, but particularly in Germany, where it continued to be played until the early nineteenth century. Arnold Dolmetsch championed its twentieth-century revival, as he did for many early instruments.

PERFORMANCE

C. P. E. BACH, the fifth son of Johann Sebastian, was an enthusiast: the sonatas and rondos in his collection *Kenner und Liebhaber* ('Connoisseurs and Amateurs') date from 1779–87. Twentieth-century composer Herbert Howells composed for the instrument, including the pragmatically titled *Howells' Clavichord*.

CONNECTIONS

The **clavinet** was a 1960s electrified version of the clavichord which produced a pleasingly gentle percussive sound.

Grand Piano

THE DEVELOPMENT of the early pianoforte into the magnificent grand piano was made possible by a number of innovations and inventions that together brought the kind of power and projection that could happily compete with the sound levels of a full orchestra or a jazz rhythm section.

A single cast-iron frame – perfected in the US – brought stability and the opportunity for more accurate tuning and better tension on the strings. The French manufacturer

An ornately decorated model.

Érard provided the 'double escapement' action, allowing for fast repetition of the same note. And laying the long bass strings over the shorter high strings ('overstringing') helped to redeploy the stress. All of these elements came together in the 1859 patent by Steinway for an iron-framed, overstrung, double-escapement grand piano.

The modern concert grand is a beautiful, impressive object and an engineering triumph: with over 10,000 parts, including those three pedals that still puzzle many a piano player – the left one mutes, the right sustains by letting all the strings resonate, and the one in the middle sustains only those notes originally held down.

PERFORMANCE

THE COLOSSAL and evolving range of the grand piano can be understood by comparing a Beethoven sonata (the formidable *Pathétique*), a Debussy piano work (the shimmering *Clair de Lune*) and a Rachmaninov concerto (such as his Third, featured in the film *Shine*). Its percussive qualities are evident in Stravinsky's *Petrushka* and Bartók's ferocious *Allegro Barbaro*. Jazz pianist Keith Jarrett explores the sonorous possibilities of the instrument in works like *The Köln Concert*, and Larry Knechtel's grand piano work is distinguished on Simon and Garfunkel's 'Bridge Over Troubled Water'.

CONNECTIONS

Examples of upright grands, with the strings running vertically so the instrument could fit against a wall, include the **giraffe piano** and **lyre piano**.

The strings and keys of a grand piano.

Classic Piano Makes

O NCE THE ESSENTIALS of the concert grand piano were in place, individual manufacturers began to assert themselves – and just as violinists have their personal preference for a Stradivarius, Guarneri or Amati, so pianists find they are drawn to the tone, action and response of a certain make.

Four of the most renowned grand piano manufacturers are:

- Bösendorfer: founded in 1828 in Vienna; the luminous clarity of their pianos' sound particularly appealed to Franz Liszt, jazz pianist Oscar Peterson and arch-perfectionists Steely Dan, who acquired a Bösendorfer for Michael Omartian to play throughout *Katy Lied*. The huge Imperial Grand has 95 rather than the standard 88 keys.

- Steinway: 1853 was a good year for pianos – Bechstein, Blüthner and Steinway all set up shop. The innovative New York-based Steinway Company (they introduced the third pedal for selective sustain) produced powerful, durable grands, and were canny marketeers, using performers like Ignacy Paderewski and Artur Rubinstein to promote their pianos. Their Model D – nigh

Advertisement for a Bechstein piano.

on nine feet (2.75 m) in length – is considered by many to be the finest concert piano ever.

- Bechstein: Carl Bechstein, a Berlin-based piano maker, saw Lizst in action at a concert and realised that the pianos of the future would have to be able to survive that level of passionate pounding. He quickly built a reputation for high quality, trustworthy pianos of an idiosyncratically ripe, clear, almost clamorous tone.

- Blüthner: the reputation of this Leipzig company spread via the alumni of the local conservatoire. Among their innovations were the addition of a sympathetic fourth string for notes in the higher register (producing a singing, silvery tone) and constructing a special light-weight piano for the ill-fated Hindenburg airship.

Rosewood baby grand, built by Steinway.

Harmonium

THE HUMBLE HARMONIUM was patented by the French company Debain in the 1840s. Its volume was limited, the number of stops few and its versatility minimal, but with the outlay of relatively little cost – and skill – a small church could acquire an organ sound; eventually heavy-weight composers such as Berlioz and Richard Strauss came to admire its qualities.

Two foot pedals were pressed up and down in turn, blowing air across the pipes; the air was transferred to a reservoir before passing through to the pipes, but the 'expression' stop gave the player the option of directly controlling the airflow with their feet, thus gaining some small compensation against their organist colleagues (the French sometimes called it the 'orgue expressif'). An alternative system, particularly common in America, sucked the air into the instrument to produce a softer tone.

The harmonium scored highly for its portability and convenience: at its peak 15,000 a year were being produced in the US for the chapel market. The instrument was also an attractive piece of home entertainment – a kind of aural Playstation – since it was easy to play and often used numbered buttons to produce the chords.

PERFORMANCE

BERLIOZ'S *Little Shepherd's Piece* and Dvořák's Bagatelles For Two Violins, Cello and Harmonium are rare examples of compositions by classical composers. Nico, in her post-Velvet Underground phase, played it mournfully on doom-laden solo albums like *The Marble Index* and *Desertshore*; a harmonium also underpins the opening of Pink Floyd's 'The Post War Dream' (from *The Final Cut*).

CONNECTIONS

The **book harmonium** was an extremely portable version developed to play while visiting presumably appreciative friends in hospital.

Harpsichord

T HE HARPSICHORD took the plucked-string concept of the virginal and spinet to new heights. The earliest example still in existence dates from the 1520s, when Italy was the major centre, but the instrument continued to develop through to the early 1800s: French harpsichords of the seventeenth and eighteenth centuries were especially graceful and elegantly decorated.

The jack-and-plectrum technique remained essentially the same as its predecessors; however the strings ran at right angles to the keyboard or manual (of which there might be two), and the strings were set in courses of two or more. Yet the harpsichord still suffered from the problem of quick decay: once a string had been plucked the note would fade too swiftly. To compensate, performers and composers added all manner of trills and other ornamentation. And to deal with the lack of dynamics, various attempts – some using a Venetian blind system – were made to boost the volume.

Ladies at the harpsichord.

Whereas the clavichord was seen primarily as a solo instrument, the harpsichord was particularly effective and important in ensemble work, providing the continuo for voices or other instruments (usually improvised from an annotated bass line).

PERFORMANCE

J. S. BACH'S Chromatic Fantasia and Fugue in D Minor is effectively a transcription of one of his astonishing improvisations; the melancholy *Tambourin* by Rameau is more meditative. For continuo work look no further than Purcell's opera *Dido and Aeneas*. More recent appearances include the Beach Boys' 'God Only Knows', the Stranglers' 'Golden Brown' and on Tori Amos's album *Boys for Pele*.

CONNECTIONS

The **clavicytherium** was an upright harpsichord, with the soundboard rising vertically above the keyboard for greater sound projection.

Organ

WAY BEFORE virginals, clavichords and spinets were dreamt of, the organ was already in its mature stage of development. Simple versions existed before the Christian era, and by the tenth century the organ was advanced enough to feature a double manual (or keyboard) and hundreds of pipes, providing the powerful swell of church music that accompanied the growth of Christianity.

At their most essential, organs are a set of pipes, sounded by air released from a windchest and controlled by valves operated by keys or foot pedals – there is power, but no touch sensitivity. The pipes fall into two distinct categories:

- Flue: sounded whenever air strikes the top lip (like a panpipes).
- Reed: where the air is vibrated by a metal tongue.

From medieval times onwards the motto of the organ was 'bigger and better', multiple manuals (including the great, swell, choir and solo) and a vast array of organ stops imitating different instruments and voices. When the French organ-maker Aristide Cavaillé-Col added the surge of electricity the volume continued to rise (a power responded to by composers like Charles-Marie Widor and Cesar Franck), up to the massive auditorium organ in Atlantic City, New Jersey, reckoned to be as loud as two dozen brass bands.

PERFORMANCE

BACH'S TOCCATA and Fugue in D Minor is a virtuoso *tour de force*. From the revival of organ composition following Cavaillé-Col's technical innovations, Franck's Chorale No. 2 in B Minor is mystically contemplative; Widor's famous Toccata (from his Fifth Organ Symphony) is known to most wedding attendees.

CONNECTIONS

The **automatic barrel organ**, using pins on pre-prepared drums to control the release of air into its flue pipes, was adopted by both country churches and street entertainers. The **regal**, or **portative organ**, was a tiny portable reed-organ popular in the fifteenth and sixteenth centuries, often used in processions.

Piano Accordion

THE PIANO ACCORDION, effectively an outsize mouth organ with bellows and a keyboard, emerged in the early nineteenth century as a Viennese invention, although its roots go back 5,000 years to the cheng, a Chinese instrument which used bamboo pipes, a gourd and a windchamber to achieve a similar effect.

The accordian in performance.

The principle of the accordion is relatively simple; by moving the bellows in and out with the left hand, air is forced through the various reeds. The left hand also presses pre-set chord buttons, while the right hand picks out the melody. The squeezebox was briefly on the verge of becoming accepted as an orchestral instrument (Tchaikovsky incorporated it in his Suite No. 2 in C Major), but the accordion's main role has always been as an extremely portable way of providing rich accompaniment to folk songs and dances.

In fact the most striking aspect of the instrument is its universality, from the cafés of France to the pubs of Galway and the klezmer bands of eastern Europe. The accordion adds an essential element to the sounds of the tango, merengue and polka, and features widely in country and cajun music.

PERFORMANCE

THE MELANCHOLY Parisian sound is best captured by
Edith Piaf recordings such as 'La Vie En Rose'. Authentic good-
time New Orleans accordion is typified by Buckwheat Zydeco's
'Ma Tit Fille'. For Irish virtuosity, Sharon Shannon's
eponymous debut album is outstanding.

CONNECTIONS

The hexagonal **concertina** beloved of hornpipe-dancing sailors has no
keyboard – just two set of studs – and is consequently deemed to be
more demanding to play. National variants of the accordion include the
Russian **bayan** and the Argentinean **bandoneon**.

Pianoforte

THE TITLE of father of the modern piano is generally credited to Bartolomeo Cristofori, who was the keeper of instruments at the court of the Florentine Medici family. Like others at the time he wanted to find a way to combine the ability of the clavichord to use crescendo and diminuendo with the brilliance and relative power of the harpsichord.

After a number of prototypes Cristofori produced his 'gravicembalo col piano e forte', or harpsichord with loud and soft, in 1709, creating an action that allowed a leather hammer to hit a string (from underneath), be caught to prevent it rebounding on to the string, and finally damp the string. The idea, though, did not initially catch on – Cristofori only made a score of pianos – until German manufacturers like Gottfried Silbermann began improving the hammer action in the 1720s. The development of the affordable square piano increased its popularity, and by the end of the eighteenth century the English Broadwood company had adopted the sustain pedal.

By the time Broadwood sent Beethoven a pianoforte in 1818, the groundwork was set for the arrival of the metal frame and the innovations that created the modern grand piano in the nineteenth century.

Caricature of the composer Franz Liszt on the pianoforte.

PERFORMANCE

PIANOFORTE WORKS that can be heard on CD, played on authentic period instruments, include Josef Haydn's Variations in F Minor, J. C. Bach's Sonata in B-flat Major Opus 17, No. 6 and Mozart's Fantasia in C. One of Cristofori's original 'pianos' from 1726 features in a recording of Giuseppe Paladini's Divertimento in G Major, performed by Walter Bernstein. The Italian composer Muzio Clementi was one of the first composers to write specifically for the pianoforte rather than the harpsichord: his *Gradus ad Parnassum* remains a seminal set of studies.

CONNECTIONS

The **orphica** – dating from around 1800 – was an extraordinary instrument designed as a portable piano and worn round the player's neck.

Upright Piano

FROM HONKY-TONK BARS to the low point of piano-smashing contests of the 1970s, the upright has been seen as the poor cousin of the grand. It can never recreate the power and tone of a grand, but its compact shape brought music into the heart of hundreds of thousands of homes at the end of the nineteenth century.

The upright piano was developed in the 1800s from what previously had been grand pianos with the strings and soundboard placed up against a wall – constructions too tall to be practical. However, two amendments made all the difference: the Austrian Matthias Müller and the American John Hawkins realised independently that if the strings started from near ground level the height would be drastically reduced – further improved by using a diagonal layout for the strings. Robert Wornum of London added the final touch in the 1830s with a tape-check action, preventing the hammer rebounding on to the strings, and still in use today.

Although the placement against a wall could lead to a lack of resonance, with the added disadvantage of the player having his or her back to the audience, or fellow musicians, the upright proved convenient and immensely popular – a vogue enhanced by the arrival in the late nineteenth century of the automated player piano, which meant that no musical skill was required for families at home to enjoy performances by the great players of the day.

PERFORMANCE

SCOTT JOPLIN'S recordings of his own 'Maple Leaf Rag' and 'The Entertainer' were most likely performed on an upright (he also produced piano rolls of his versions), Jelly Roll Morton's 'Jelly Roll Blues' and 'King Porter Stomp' likewise.

CONNECTIONS

The **player piano** or **pianola** is an automatic upright, which uses air pressure controlled by the holes in a paper roll to control the striking of hammers against the piano's strings.

Virginal

ONE OF THE OLDEST of the string keyboard instruments, the virginal dates from as early as the 1460s and marks the beginning of the harpsichord family. Its generally oblong case was often highly decorated, particularly the back of the lid, which might display an intricately painted landscape on being lifted up, revealing a small three- to four-octave keyboard with strings running parallel – the particular characteristic of the virginal.

The instrument was played on a table or laid across the performer's lap. To produce its clear, articulate and brilliant sound, the strings were plucked: as a key was pressed down, its jack would be raised, simultaneously lifting a damper clear and pushing a plectrum against the string, which could vibrate until the player took his – or more likely her – finger off the key.

Playing the virginal was considered part of the skills of an educated young woman (hence the instrument's name, according to some sources) and was particularly important in English music of the early seventeenth century. The concept was developed into the spinet – which frequently had a wing-shaped body more like a grand piano, strings set at 45 degrees to the keyboard and a fuller tone.

PERFORMANCE

WALSINGHAM, the set of 30 variations by the virtuoso virginalist John Bull, and William Byrd's *The Woods So Wild* are among the nearly 300 pieces collected in the *Fitzwilliam Virginal Book*, the main depository of English music for the virginal.

CONNECTIONS

The **chekker** was the first term used for string keyboard instruments, but experts seem unable to decide whether this was a precursor of the virginal, a clavichord or an upright harpsichord.

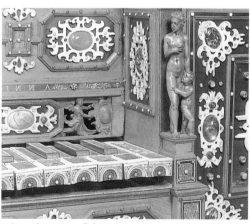

Sixteenth-century jewelled spinet.

ELECTRONIC INSTRUMENTS
Introduction

THE TERM 'ELECTRONIC' is used here to describe every kind of instrument that involves electrical or electronic means to produce or amplify musical sounds. This section covers the following types of electronic instrument.

ELECTRIC ORGAN

FROM THE 1920s various inventors were developing their own versions of the electric organ, using electronic circuits and mechanical techniques to produce notes. The electric organ that has achieved the widest acceptance is the Hammond organ.

ELECTRIC PIANO

THE EARLIEST types of electric piano were developed in the 1960s. Led by the Fender Rhodes and the Wurlitzer, these keyboards were intended to be portable versions of the pianoforte and became very popular during the 1970s in many styles of popular music.

SYNTHESIZER

ELECTRONIC DEVICES, such as the theremin of 1920, had been made earlier in the century, but it was not until the 1950s that the first sophisticated synthesizer, the RCA Mk I, was built. Subsequent miniaturisation and digital technology has made such instruments much smaller and more versatile.

SAMPLERS AND DRUM MACHINES

THE FIRST practical electronic sampler, the prohibitively expensive Fairlight CMI, appeared in the late 1970s. Since then, such devices have become less expensive and are widely heard on modern popular music. Drum machines have become an important aspect of popular music-making since their rise in popularity in the early 1980s. They are electronic devices that can produce highly complex rhythms in a continuous sequence.

ELECTRIC GUITAR

THE HISTORY of the electric guitar dates back to early experiments in the 1930s at the Rickenbacker guitar company. With the development of a vast range of guitars, led by the Fender and Gibson companies, it has become probably the twentieth century's most characteristic instrument and a defining sound of its music.

BASS GUITAR

THE ELECTRIC bass guitar, starting with Fender's 1951 Precision, has replaced the double bass and become an essential instrument in many popular music styles.

Bass Guitar

I N 1951, GUITAR MAKER Leo Fender launched the first commercially available electric bass guitar, the Fender Precision. Compared to the cumbersome and often difficult-to-hear acoustic double bass, Fender offered an instrument that had many advantages. Not only was it louder because it was amplified – and more portable – it allowed for more precise intonation because the neck was fretted. Country-and-western players were among the first to adopt the Precision, and during the 1950s and 1960s the bass guitar became established as a mainstay of all styles of modern music making. Four strings tuned E, A, D and G are usual, although a few models with five or more strings are made.

The design principles of the Fender bass guitars have stood the test of time remarkably well: a solid body, larger machine-heads to cope with heavier strings, one or two electro-magnetic pickups, and a bolt-on neck. Fender went on to introduce the Jazz Bass in 1960 and other less successful models. Apart from notable exceptions such as the Rickenbacker 4001S (1964) and the Gibson Thunderbird IV (1964), the electric basses of other big guitar companies never gained the broad acceptance of the Fenders. From the 1970s' specialist bass makers such as Ampeg, Alembic and Wal began to cater for more discerning players.

The Fender-based style of construction went unchallenged until Ned Steinberger brought out his radical innovation in the early 1980s: a bass guitar with no headstock and a tiny body. He did this by using reinforced epoxy resin (claimed to be stronger and lighter than steel) instead of wood, and by putting the tuning mechanisms at the other end of the body.

PERFORMANCE

THE FENDER Jazz is played fretless by Jaco Pastorius on 'Night Passage' by Weather Report. Hear the technical twang of Chris Squire's Rickenbacker on Yes's *The Yes Album*. You can see and hear Paul McCartney play his Hofner 'Violin Bass' in the film *Let it Be*.

CONNECTIONS

The related **acoustic bass guitar**, which looks like an oversize acoustic guitar, is rarely played.

Electric Guitar

I F ONE INSTRUMENT can claim to be the twentieth century's greatest, then the electric guitar is probably it. When the early pioneers, Adolph Rickenbacker, George Beauchamp and Paul Barth, experimented with electro-magnetic pickups to amplify the sound of a guitar in the 1930s, none could have foreseen what an impact this innovation would have on all styles of popular music.

In the mid 1930s, Charlie Christian was one of the first to see the potential as a soloist of playing a guitar that could be

heard properly in a jazz band. He played an early 'Electric Spanish' ES-150 guitar made by Gibson. For generations of jazz players, the mellow clarity of the electric-acoustic guitar became a traditional and characteristic sound.

Early rock'n'roll records, such as Bill Haley and the Comets' 1954 hit 'Rock Around the Clock' kick-started the electric guitar's mass appeal. Rock'n'rollers like Chuck Berry exploited the chugging rhythmic capability of semi-acoustic instruments from the late

Jimi Hendrix.

1950s into the 1960s. From the early 1960s, countless groups, led by The Beatles and The Rolling Stones, based their music around the electric guitar.

The advent in the late 1960s of very loud blues-influenced rock music saw the flowering of the solid electric guitar, led by the hugely influential Jimi Hendrix playing a Fender Stratocaster. The popularity of electric guitars was renewed in the 1990s with the success of groups like Nirvana and Oasis.

PERFORMANCE

ON HIS *Electric Ladyland*, Jimi Hendrix's inspired experimentation with fuzz, feedback and wah-wah effects expanded the sound world of the electric guitar. Jazz maestro Joe Pass demonstrates his mastery on *Virtuoso*. The soaring blues of B. B. King is captured live on *Live At The Regal*.

CONNECTIONS

Guitar synthesizers enable a guitarist to trigger a synthesizer through a pitch-to-voltage connector. Notable models have been produced by Korg and Roland.

Classic Electric Guitars

SINCE THE 1930s, the history of the electric guitar has been one of enormous growth and variety. Here is a selection of classic models, treasured by players and collectors alike for their superior design and workmanship.

Fender Stratocaster (1954): possibly the greatest and most emulated instrument, it features a vibrato arm and three pickups offering unrivalled tone variety.

Fender Telecaster (1951): this simple solid two-pickup guitar has a distinctive bridge/pickup unit and its hard clear sound is a perennial favourite for country and rock players.

Gibson Les Paul (1952): the guitarist and inventor Les Paul contributed much of the design of this highly carved solid body guitar, prized for its full sustain.

Gibson ES-335 (1958): a classic double-cutaway design, combining a hollow body with a solid centre block to give more sustain and less feedback.

Gretsch White Falcon (1955): this ostentatious white model with two pickups and a Bigsby vibrato arm was one of many electric acoustic models produced.

Rickenbacker 360-12 (1964): this distinctive 12-string guitar was featured on many recordings by The Beatles and The Byrds.

PERFORMANCE

THE BYRDS' 'Mr Tambourine Man' highlights the rich jangle of the 12-string Rickenbacker. With his Gibson Les Paul, Jimmy Page excels at extended rock solos on *Led Zeppelin II*. Jimi Hendrix displays the tender side of the Fender Stratocaster on 'Little Wing'.

CONNECTIONS

Some vintage guitars produced by other manufacturers such as Epiphone, Guild, Vox and Hofner are rated as 'cult' classics by collectors.

Fender Stratocaster.

Electric Organ

THE ELECTRIC ORGAN emerged in the early twentieth century, originally designed as an economical and compact substitute for the larger pipe organ. During its history, makers have employed various techniques for producing tones: vibrating reeds, spinning tone wheels, oscillator circuits and digital samplers. Notable early examples include the French *Orgue des Ondes* ('Wave Organ'), developed in the late 1920s by Edouard Coupleux and Armand Givelet, the 'Radio Organ of a Trillion Tones' and the Rangertone of the early 1930s.

Probably the most well-known is the Hammond organ, patented by its American inventor Laurens Hammond in 1934. Featuring two keyboards and a set of foot pedals, it produces its unmistakable sound through a set of rotary generators, using drawbars to produce a great variety of tone colours. The Hammond swirling through a Leslie rotating speaker cabinet

was at the heart of much black American music from the 1960s onward, especially gospel, jazz, blues and funk.

By the 1960s valves in electric organs had given way to transistors, which were superseded

Left and right: Examples of the Hammond organ.

in turn by microcircuits in the 1970s. Instead of originating notes internally, the latest types play digitally-stored samples (see Sampler and Drum Machine, p. 158), allowing players to imitate almost any other instrument.

PERFORMANCE

CHECK OUT Jimmy Smith's exuberant funky grooves on his soul-jazz album, *Back at the Chicken Shack*. Spooner Oldham's soulful, gospel-influenced playing on many of Aretha Franklin's classic Atlantic recordings was the inspiration for one of today's leading players, Larry Goldings. Procul Harum's atmospheric 'A Whiter Shade of Pale' had a famous Bach theme (the air from his orchestral Suite No. 3) at its heart.

CONNECTIONS

Made in 1904, American inventor Thaddeus Cahill's 200-ton, keyboard-operated **telharmonium** was an important precursor to the electronic organ.

Electric Piano

THE ELECTRIC PIANO can sound smooth and mellow, hard and funky, or anywhere in between. Its popularity peaked in the 1970s and declined during the 1980s, only to find a new generation of fans in the worlds of acid-jazz, hip-hop, and garage. Although the Yamaha CP70 electric grand became widely accepted and a new generation of digital pianos has emerged, for many players there were only two main makes to choose from: the Fender Rhodes or the Wurlitzer.

FENDER RHODES

MOST INFLUENTIAL in the 1970s, the 'Rhodes' helped define the sound of jazz-funk and jazz-fusion, and was played by many soul, funk and disco artists.

Harold Rhodes developed his Army Air Corps Piano from old bits salvaged from B-17 bombers. Using no electrics at all, he achieved a compact portable piano by using aluminium pipes instead of strings. In the late 1950s, Rhodes collaborated with guitar maker Leo Fender to make the 32-note Piano Bass model, made famous by Ray Manzarek of The Doors. The famous 72-note Suitcase model, introduced in 1965, was the first one with the unique 'real' Rhodes sound.

WURLITZER

FREQUENTLY MORE at home in a guitar-based rock or pop band, the 'Wurly' has enjoyed great success from the early 1960s onwards.

The Wurlitzer's development started when the Everett piano company experimented with B. F. Meissner's ideas about electro-magnetic pickups. The giant American jukebox and theatre organ manufacturer, Wurlitzer, then applied this pickup technology to make an amplifiable piano in which hammers strike metal reeds and the Wurlitzer electric piano was born. The popular EP200 model was first made in the early 1960s.

PERFORMANCE

THE HARD jangling attack of the Wurlitzer can be heard on 'Dreamer' by Supertramp and 'You're My Best Friend' by Queen. For the cleaner, more lyrical sound of the Rhodes, listen to the soulful Donny Hathaway on 'Everything is Everything' or the clarity of Elton John's classic 'Daniel'.

CONNECTIONS

Unsurprisingly, the **electric piano** is closely related to the conventional piano. Players of electric pianos often also play **synthesizers**.

Sampler and Drum Machine

AS WITH THE latest synthesizers, a sampler uses digital technology to make sounds. The difference is that, instead of generating an original synthetic sound, it actually 'plays' a mini digital recording of a sound. This could be anything – a voice, a drum beat or even a milk bottle being dropped! In the late 1970s, a pioneering sampling musical instrument such as the Fairlight CMI was as expensive as a Ferrari sports car. By the mid 1990s, samplers were no more expensive than regular synthesizers. In the future, it is likely that dedicated hardware samplers will be forsaken for more versatile personal computers that can do the same thing.

Many people use samples from CDs or download them from the Internet. Others prefer to make their own, using the sampler to make a digital recording of the sound they want (often from other people's records). Either way, the sample can then be played musically by connecting a keyboard to the sampler.

An electronic keyboard allows a sound to be played from the sampler.

Drum machines have changed the approach to providing rhythm in music. There are two types: the type that produces a continuous beat to a pre-set pattern, and those that are played in 'real time' using sticks. A key example of the first type is Roland's TR-606 Drumatix, introduced in 1981, which inspired a generation of dance-music mixers and audiences. Roger Linn's LinnDrum, launched in 1986, is an influential instrument of the second type. It makes sampled drum sounds when special pads are hit.

PERFORMANCE

'TRANS-EUROPE EXPRESS' by synthesizer pioneers Kraftwerk was one of the most sampled records of the 1980s; its sounds were copied by many artists, notably Afrika Bambaataa on their 'Planet Rock'.

CONNECTIONS

An important related piece of studio technology is the **sequencer**, a device programmed to trigger sequences of notes or beats on a linked synthesizer or sampler.

Synthesizer

THE SYNTHESIZER has come a long way since the world's first one – the American RCA Mk I, made in 1951, whose bulk occupied a laboratory. To play it, composers such as Milton Babbitt (who was a fan of Mk II) had to tap in punched tape instructions – there was no keyboard. Synthesizers became commercially available during the mid-1960s when two innovators, Donald Buchla and Robert Moog, each brought out their own designs. Robert Moog's Moog, with its new voltage-controlled oscillator, was the more influential and was played by top rock keyboard players such as Keith Emerson.

A conventional synthesizer is a keyboard instrument that generates a wide variety of sounds purely electronically, using no mechanical parts at all. With many models providing pre-programmed sounds as well as the capability of altering every aspect of a sound (e.g. pitch, timbre, attack and delay), the synthesizer player can imitate a range of instruments or invent entirely new squeaks, warbles or rumbles.

Analogue synthesizers are now regarded as classics and are collected for the unique quality of their sounds. From the late 1970s, these gave way to a new generation that used digital microcomputers, for example the Fairlight CMI (which plays sampled sounds (see p. 158) and Yamaha's FM (frequency modulation) models.

PERFORMANCE

WALTER (NOW WENDY) Carlos pioneered the early Moog with technical precision on *Switched on Bach*. 'Autobahn' by the German band Kraftwerk inspired the late 1970s synthesizer boom. Listen to The Human League's 'Don't You Want Me Baby?' for their influential 1980s synthesizer band sound.

CONNECTIONS

Modern digital synthesizers are played in conjunction with **samplers**, **sequencers** and other studio equipment, using MIDI (Musical Instrument Digital Interface) to connect them together.

Synthesizers are often played with other digital studio equipment.

INVENTIONS AND ODDITIES

Introduction

SINCE THE beginning of time, humans have been highly inventive and resourceful in finding and making new ways to communicate using sounds. This has usually involved taking materials or technology to hand and creating something new out of them. Just as early ancestors fashioned flutes from hollow bones, so more recent innovators have used electronic machines to make music. This section gives a selective survey of inventions and music-making devices – some may be familiar, some unusual and some just plain odd.

As well as being a vital part of our musical heritage, the sound of the human voice has been used and adapted in unusual ways in the twentieth century. In addition to the familiar instruments heard in classical and modern music, there are a multitude of musical oddities from around the world. During the twentieth century, inventors have seized upon the musical possibilities of the mechanical and electrical technologies around them and made strange and wonderful contraptions. The attentive listener to recorded and live music will sometimes hear unfamiliar sound effects, called for by the composer to evoke a particular mood or idea. One of the most significant techniques of the twentieth century was musique concrète, which was a precursor to modern-day sampling technology.

Wind machine.

The Voice

THE HUMAN VOICE is our primeval musical instrument, with our earliest ancestors finding expression through their voices before thought was ever given to other sources of sound. Vocal music has been sung from the beginnings of recorded history; the Sumerians sang in their temples 5,000 years ago. In the West, traditions of singing have evolved from the plainchant of the middle ages, through seventeenth-century opera to today's various music styles. Rather than survey the vast history of vocal music, this section considers some of the ususual uses to which the voice has been put.

PERFORMANCE

ELLA FITZGERALD was probably the most accomplished jazz singer of the twentieth century. She was highly skilled at 'scat' singing, in which sung jazz phrases can resemble instruments such as the saxophone. This technique can be heard on many of her records. Dee Dee Bridgewater is also an outstanding modern exponent of this style of singing.

The avant-garde performance artist Laurie Anderson had

an unexpected UK hit record in 1981 with 'O Superman', a part-spoken, part-sung hypnotic intonation using a digital vocoder device to shift the pitch of her voice.

With his 1976 hit 'Show Me the Way', the pop-rock guitarist Peter Frampton used a novel 'voice tube' effect unit that allowed him to alter the tone of his guitar by changing the shape of his mouth.

CONNECTIONS

Wendy Carlos famously used a **vocoder**, a synthesizer that uses voices to influence the quality of the sounds, to compose 'Timesteps' for the soundtrack (also available on CD) of Stanley Kubrick's film *A Clockwork Orange*.

Left: Jazz singer Ella Fitzgerald.

Oddities

The history of music making includes a vast range
of unusual, sometimes obscure, instruments. Many
of these demonstrate the sheer serendipitous
imagination of their inventors. A selection of some
of the more interesting and surprising of these
oddities is given below.

GLASS ARMONICA

IRISHMAN Richard Pockrich excelled on this instrument in
1743. It is played by rubbing wetted fingers on the rims of
glasses set in a frame, each glass being filled with a different
quantity of water to tune its pitch. Benjamin Franklin's version
of 1761 used a treadle to operate a revolving row of glass discs
half-immersed in a water tray to keep them moist. Mozart's
Quintet in C minor, K617, includes musical glasses.

JINGLING JOHNNY

ALSO CALLED a Turkish crescent or a Chinese pavilion, this
exotic instrument possibly originated from the staff of a Central
Asian shaman. Part of the Turkish military band sound that
stimulated the late eighteenth-century European vogue for
Turkish music, it consists of a long vertical pole hung with bells
fixed to crescent-shaped cross pieces. Haydn is thought to have
specified it for his 'Military' Symphony No. 100.

THUMB PIANO

ALSO CALLED a sansa, zeze or likembe, the thumb piano is
an African musical instrument consisting of a set of tuned metal

or bamboo strips of different lengths fastened to a soundboard. It sometimes has an attached resonator box or can be played inside a gourd to improve its sound. As the name suggests, the tuned strips are depressed and released by thumb or finger to give a liquid twangy sound.

BULL ROARER

THIS MOST ancient of instruments is played by many peoples such as Aboriginals in Australia and Inuit in the Arctic. It is typically made from flat wood, at least 15 cm in length, with a shape incorporating notches on one edge. This is attached by a cord and swung above the head, making an unearthly roaring buzz, thought by ancient users to invoke magic powers, and more recently included in the Australian ballet score *Corroboree* of 1946.

Musical glasses.

Twentieth-century Inventions

The twentieth century saw an unprecedented explosion in new machines for making sound. Here is a selection of the most important and influential of such instruments.

INTONARUMORI

LUIGI RUSSOLO was a member of the Italian Futurists, who made art and objects to celebrate the new industrial machine age. Between 1913 and 1921 Russolo and Ugo Piatti designed a range of intonarumori ('noise intoners'), that made various rumbles, crashes, booms and shrieks, many produced by turning a handle.

THEREMIN

INVENTED IN 1920 by the Russian Leon Theremin, this instrument consists of a box containing thermionic valves producing oscillations, with antenna protruding from it. An expressive, ethereal continuous tone is produced, whose pitch can be altered by moving the hand towards and away from the antenna. Brian Wilson of the Beach Boys featured it on 'Good Vibrations'.

ONDES MARTENOT

ALSO CALLED Ondes Musicales ('musical waves'), this electronic musical instrument was first demonstrated in 1928 by the French

Modern version of a theremin.

inventor Maurice Martenot. Inside, thermionic valves produce oscillating frequencies in a similar way to the theremin. The latest version could alter the pitch using a keyboard. The composer Messiaen used its disembodied vocal-like sounds in his *Turangalila* Symphony.

TRAUTONIUM

ASSISTED BY Oskar Sala who became the instrument's virtuoso, the German Friedrich Trautwein introduced the trautonium in 1930. Tones were produced by touching a fingerboard, altering the pitch of the oscillation which was then amplified through a loudspeaker. The composer Paul Hindemith was inspired to write a Concertina for Trautonium and Orchestra.

MELLOTRON

THE MELLOTRON was a keyboard instrument produced in England between 1963 and 1986. Depressing a key played a sound of up to eight seconds recorded on a magnetic tape. The

Mellotron made a unique and instantly recognisable sound that became popular with 1960s and 1970s groups. The Moody Blues showed its symphonic side on *Every Good Boy Deserves Favour*. Listen out for it in the Sci-Fi film *The Day the Earth Stood Still*.

Unusual Effects

In an orchestral setting, it traditionally falls to the percussionist to contribute any special effects required for the music. Here are just a few of the unlikely contraptions that have found their way into musical scores.

- Bird Scare: a kind of rattle formerly found on every football terrace, it occurs in Havergal Brian's Symphony No. 1 (1927).

- Cannon: the best-known occurrence of cannon is in Tchaikovsky's *1812* Overture.

- Chains: these can be shaken and dragged, and are called for in Schoenberg's *Gurrelieder* (1901).

- Sandpaper: the rarely heard effect of rubbed sheets of sandpaper is featured in the *Sandpaper Ballet* (1954) by Leroy Anderson.

- Saw: popular in early twentieth-century music hall, this is played with a bow.

Several composers have specified it, notably Toshiro Mayuzumi in his *Tone Pleromas 55* (1955).

- Spoons: a pair of ordinary spoons clicked together was a popular music hall turn and is heard in George Auric's ballet *Les Matelots* (1924).

- Thunder sheet: the orchestral version uses a thin metal sheet, agitated by soft mallets. John Cage wanted five of them in his *First Construction* (1942).

- Typewriter: in the early twentieth century, this sound was heard in every office. Eric Satie in his *Parade* (1917) was one of several composers who wanted its percussive effect.

Thunder sheet (opposite) and sandpaper blocks.

Musique Concrète

In April 1948, Pierre Schaeffer, a technician at the
Radiodiffusion Française in Paris, conceived his
Etude aux chemins de fer ('Study for trains') – it was
the first piece of musique concrète. This innovative
kind of music represented a new direction in music-
making, distinct from earlier uses of electronic or
mechanical machines to generate sounds.

MUSIQUE CONCRÈTE was an experimental technique
that combined pre-recorded sounds – natural as well as
musical – to make musical compositions. Using only the
earliest tape recorders, sounds were edited, played backwards
and speeded up and down to create fascinating 'sound-scapes'.
Pierre Henry was a prolific composer of musique concrète
and collaborated with Schaeffer on many compositions.
Luciano Berio and Steve Reich are also key figures in musique
concrète composition. Karlheinz Stockhausen combined
electronic and concrète sounds to become a leader of avant-
garde music making.

Four important studios were established for further
experimentation in the areas of musique concrète and
electronic music:

● Columbia-Princeton Electronic Music Center, New York.
Founded in 1951 by Vladimir Ussachevsky and Otto
Luening.

- Studio für Elektronische Musik, Cologne. Used primarily to make electronically generated music, it was established by Herbert Eimert in 1951.
- Studio di Fonologia, Milan. Established in 1953, it was used by many avant-garde composers: Berio, Pousseur, Nono, Maderna and Cage.
- Institut de Recherche et de Coordination Acoustique/Musique (IRCAM), Paris. Established in 1976, this is a major centre for creativity and research in sound.

PERFORMANCE

VARÈSE'S *POÈME ÉLECTRONIQUE* was performed by 400 loudspeakers at the 1958 Brussels World's Fair. Luciano Berio produced a celebrated piece, *Thema* (1958), using his wife Cathy Berberian's voice reading from James Joyce's *Ulysses*. One of the best-known compositions by Schaeffer and Henry is *Le voyage* (1961–62). Steve Reich's *Come Out* (1966) loops spoken phrases to disturbing effect.

Pierre Henry, French composer and acoustical inventor.

CONNECTIONS

The **RCA Mk II** music synthesizer, the most advanced of its time, was transferred to the Columbia-Princeton Electronic Music Center in the late 1950s.

COMPENDIUM

Ensemble Layouts

18th-Century Orchestra

In Mozart's day, the orchestra was led by the harpsichord player.

Trumpets		Timpani
Flutes	Oboes	Horns
Cellos	Violas	
Bassoons		Basses
Violins 1	Harpsichord	Violins 2

Modern Orchestra

Typical layout of a modern orchestra at full strength.

Percussion	Timpani	Trombones	Tuba
	Horns	Trumpets	
Harp	Clarinets	Bassoons	Double Basses
	Flutes	Oboes	
2nd Violins		Violas	Cellos
1st Violins	Conductor		

Big Band Jazz Orchestra

In this layout, musicians traditionally
move centre-stage to play solos.

Trumpets

Guitar

Drums

Trombones

Double Bass

Saxophones

Piano

Soloist
position

Recording Studio

The musicians will typically record
their parts separately.

Recording
equipment

Digital effects unit

Control Room

Playback
Speaker

Mixing Desk

Playback
Speaker

soundproof glass

Elec. Piano
&
Synthesizers

Vocalist

Elec.
Bass
Guitar

Studio

Elec.
Guitar

Amplifier

Drum Kit

Soundproof Booth

Percussion

Instrument Ranges

Instrument Ranges

This section shows the ranges that can be played on instruments used in modern performance. Notes above middle 'c' are named in lowercase and show the octaves proceeding higher as c¹, c² etc. Notes below middle 'c' are named in uppercase, showing the octaves proceeding lower as C, C₁, C₂ etc.

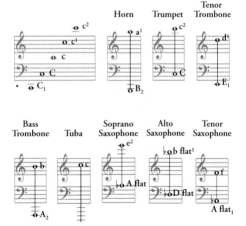

Pitches in C   Brass Instruments

Woodwind Instruments

Recorders (lowest notes)

Soprano   Alto   Tenor   Bass

Flute   Piccolo   Oboe   Cor anglais

Oboe
d'amore   Clarinet
in B♭   Clarinet
in A   Bassoon

Stringed Instruments

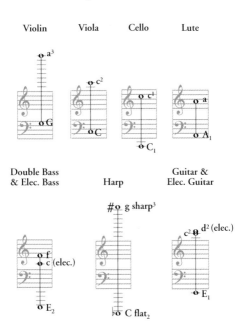

Keyboard Instruments

Technological advances have given keyboard instruments wider ranges.

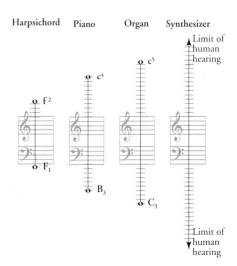

Glossary

Accidental: A sharp, flat or natural note that is not part of the key signature.

Acoustic: Not amplified or reproduced by electric or electronic means.

Allegro: A musical instruction meaning 'brisk and lively'.

Alto: High voice, above tenor, or equivalent range in instruments.

Arpeggio: From the Italian verb meaning 'to play the harp', the notes of a chord played in sequence in quick succession, with a rippling effect.

Bagatelle: A light piece of music, not taking itself too seriously.

Baritone: The second lowest adult male voice, or equivalent range in instruments.

Bass: The lowest adult male voice, or equvalent range in instruments.

Bluegrass music: US country music, usually without percussion, and featuring the banjo, fiddle and guitar.

Bore: The diameter of a wind or brass instrument's tube.

Bridge: A thin piece of hardwood supporting the strings of an instrument and transmitting their vibrations to the soundboard.

Calypso: West Indian folk song style.

Chord: A group of three or more notes sounded simultaneously.

Chromatic: Music that uses all 12 notes of the octave, or moves in intervals of one semitone.

Continuo: An annotated bass line indicating, to a keyboard (usually harpsichord) player or small group, which harmonies to improvise over, usually in Baroque music.

Crescendo: A musical instruction meaning 'increasing in volume'.

Crook: A tube, usually curved, that is added to a wind or brass instrument to alter its pitch.

Damper: A device (usually a felt pad) that mutes the vibrations of keyboard strings after the note has been played.

Diminuendo: Instruction meaning 'decreasing in volume'.

Dixieland: Early jazz style, particularly from New Orleans.

Embouchure: The application of the lips and tongue in playing a wind or brass instrument.

Ensemble: A small group of musicians, usually playing chamber music.

Escapement: Part of a piano action that lets a hammer drop away from the string after striking it, even if the note is held down.

Feedback: High-pitched whistle produced when a guitar or microphone is too near its amplifier speaker.

Fingerboard: The wooden section of e.g. a violin or guitar against which the strings are stopped by the player's fingers.

Flam: A drum beat with a brief skipping beat played immediately before it.

Flat: Indicating a note, or the sound it makes, that has been lowered in pitch by one semitone.

Fret: A metal or wooden ridge on the fingerboard of an instrument indicating where to press the finger for a particular note.

Fugue: Piece of music where a main theme is played and then repeated, varied and inter-changed, weaving the theme into a complex tapestry of sound.

Gamelan: Indonesian musical ensemble featuring gongs, drums and cymbals, with wind and string instruments.

Glissando: A continuous sliding sound typically produced by a trombone or sliding a finger up or down a violin string, or sweeping the hand across a harp's strings.

Harmonics: Individual sounds present as part of an ordinary note, present because strings or air columns can vibrate producing more than one part to the sound.

Harmony: A collection of notes sounded simultaneously, usually implying a pleasing sound.

Headstock: The top of an electric guitar neck that holds the metal tuning keys (machine heads).

Hook: The main, oft repeated, musical phrase of (particularly) a hit song.

Interval: The difference of pitch between two notes, calculated by counting the number of notes of the scale between them (e.g. the interval between C and G is a 5th).

Jack: The part of a keyboard mechanism that transmits movement to the hammer, quill or tangent.

Key: The dominant tonal range of a piece of music, relating to the notes of a particular major or minor scale e.g. 'in the key of G major'.

Key signature: A group of sharp or flat symbols at the beginning of each staff, indicating in which key a piece should be played.

Ledger line: The line placed above or below the staff to indicate notes of pitches above or below the staff.

Melody: The tune of a piece of music, a succession of notes forming a distinctive sequence.

Middle C: The note graphically represented on the the first ledger line below the treble staff or above the bass staff. When designating ranges of instruments, this note is given as 'c'.

Octave: The interval between two notes, one of twice the pitch of the other, lying eight notes away from it in the scale.

Paradiddle: A variation on a straight drum roll where the left and right hand sticks are used in the sequence LRLL RLRR LRLL.

Pavan: A slow, stately sixteeenth-century dance.

Peg-box: The part of the head of a stringed instrument which holds the tuning pegs.

Pianissimo: A musical instruction meaning 'very soft'.

Pitch: The position of a sound in the scale, how high or low it is, identified by a series of letters.

Pizzicato: Plucking the strings with the fingers (for stringed instruments normally played with a bow).

Plectrum: A small device (now usually hard plastic) for plucking the strings of an instrument.

Portamento: Playing two different notes with virtually no gap between them, almost a slide.

Reed: The vibrating, sound-producing part or tongue of a woodwind instrument or organ-pipe.

Register: The note range of a voice or instrument.

Resin: The hard substance from distilled oil of turpentine used to add edge to the bows of violins and similar stringed instruments.

Resonator: The part of an instrument that helps amplify its sound.

Rim shot: The technique of using a drumstick to strike the skin and the metal rim of a snare drum at the same time, producing a sharp crack.

Scale: A group of notes played in ascending or descending order.

Semitone: The smallest interval in standard Western music: the interval between two adjacent notes on a keyboard.

Sharp: Indicating a note, or the sound it makes, that has been raised in pitch by one semitone.

Skiffle band: Folk meets rock'n'roll in the 1950s and early 1960s, usually played on double bass, side drum, guitar and washboard.

Soprano: The highest adult female voice, or equivalent range in instruments.

Soundhole: An opening made into an instrument's sound-board (e.g. the f-hole on a violin or the circular hole on an acoustic guitar).

Staccato: From the Italian word meaning 'to separate', each note played crisply and separately.

Staff: System of five lines and four spaces on which music is written.

Syncopation: Stressing the off-beat or any beat that would not normally be accented.

Tenor: The male voice between alto and baritone, or equivalent range in instruments.

Timbre: The characteristic tone quality or colour of an instrument's sound.

Toccata: An fast, improvisatory work, particularly on the organ, showing off the player's skill (from the Italian for 'to touch').

Tone: Sound, usually referring to pitch, quality or volume.

Transpose: To move a note or series of notes upwards or downwards in pitch.

Treble: A high voice, can refer to male or female.

Tremolando/Tremolo: A trembling effect, achieved either by playing the same note rapidly or bending a held note up and down in pitch.

Tuning pegs: A peg which has the string of an instrument wrapped round it and which can be turned to adjust the pitch of the string.

Vibrato: A rapid fluctuation of a note's pitch, which a violinist creates by rocking the finger on the string.

Virtuoso: A musician of outstanding technical brilliance.

Bibliography and Acknowledgements

Bacon, Tony, *The Ultimate Guitar Book*, London, 1991

Baines, A., *Brass Instruments: Their History and Development*, Dover, 1993

Briscoe, Desmond, *The BBC Radiophonic Workshop*, London, 1983

Chapman, Richard, *The Complete Guitarist*, London, 1993

Dearling, Robert, *The Encyclopedia of Musical Instruments*, London, 1996

Griffiths, Paul, *Modern Music*, London, 1996

Holland, James, *Percussion*, London, 1992

Menuhin, Yehudi and William Primrose, *Violin & Viola*, London, 1991

Nicholls, Geoff, *The Drum Book*, 1997

Piston, Walter, *Orchestration*, London, 1978

Priestley, B., D. Gelly, P. Trynka and T. Bacon, *The Sax & Brass Book*, 1998

Sadie, Stanley (ed.), *The Cambridge Music Guide*, Cambridge, 1985

Scholes, Percy A. (orig.), *Concise Oxford Dictionary of Music*, Oxford, 1952

Summerfield, Maurice J., *The Jazz Guitar*, Gateshead, 1978

Philip Dodd would like to thank Mark and Pam Gibbon, Barry McRae, Alan Stuart, John Telfer and David Temple for their help and suggestions, and Esther and Arthur Dodd for opening up the world of music in the first place. **Ian Powling** would like to thank Fred for all his help and assistance.

Picture Credits

Arbiter Group plc: 17, 19, 25, 32, 57, 91 (r), 98, 151, 160, 161. Fender Musical Instruments Inc. 6, 148, 149, 152-3. Millennium Products 21. **Bournemouth Orchestras:** Mark David Hill 34. **Chris Stock:** 12, 14, 15, 22, 23, 31, 38, 43, 47, 49, 113, 163, 168, 170, 171. **Christie's Images:** 61, 86, 93, 117, 120-121, 69, 124, 128, 135, 141. **Hobgoblin Music:** 73, 83, 97, 108, 139. **J. D. Chapman:** 136, 137. **Lebrecht:** 35, 31, 36, 53, 62, 66, 69, 107, 114, 126, 130, 144, 173. R. Booth 111. David Farrell 110. C. R. Henderson 67. J. McCook 133. Kate Mount 89. Odile Noel 13, 26, 48, 58. F. Noranha 30, 71(t). M. Peric 16. Wladimir Polak 116. Graham Salter 11, 29, 99, 122, 167. Chris Stock 10, 27, 36, 37, 59, 76, 129, 131. **Mary Evans Picture Library:** 45, 75, 36 (b), 94, 96, 104, 127, 134, 140. **Redferns:** 8, 51. Balafon Archive 155. Chuck Boyd 7, 150. Henrietta Butler 68, 92. Graham Diss 28. Jill Douglas 154. Brigitte Engl 85(t). David Farrell 9, 100, 119. Suzi Gibbons 106. Mick Hutson 55, 72, 78, 168. Airto Moreira 33. Leon Morris 79. Odile Noel 103, 169. Outline 54. Mike Prior 18. David Redfern 20, 39, 41, 44, 60, 63, 64, 65, 73(b), 74, 82, 102, 112, 118, 138, 146, 164. Graham Salter 42, 105. Barbara Steinwehe 101. **Victoria & Albert Museum:** 109, 142, 143, 145.**Yamaha-Kemble Music (UK) Ltd:** 80-81, 84, 87, 157, 158. All graphics courtesy of Foundry Arts.

Index

COLLINS GEM
BABIES' names

COLLINS GEM
BEER

COLLINS GEM
BIRDS

COLLINS GEM
CALORIE Counter

COLLINS GEM
FACT FILE

COLLINS GEM
FENG SHUI

COLLINS GEM
FLAGS

COLLINS GEM
Healthy EATING

COLLINS GEM
QUOTATIONS

COLLINS GEM
SAS Self-Defence

COLLINS GEM
SAS Survival Guide

COLLINS GEM
SEASHORE

COLLINS GEM
TREES

COLLINS GEM
Understanding DREAMS

COLLINS GEM
WILD flowers

COLLINS GEM
WINE Dictionary